Don Weekes

SHOOTOUT
Hockey
TRIVIA

GREYSTONE BOOKS
Douglas & McIntyre Publishing Group
Vancouver/Toronto/Berkeley

To all the hockey moms and dads, who get up early and drive many miles to sit on cold arena benches and keep the game alive.

Greystone Books
A division of Douglas & McIntyre Ltd.
2323 Quebec Street, Suite 201
Vancouver, British Columbia
Canada V5T 4S7
www.greystonebooks.com

Library and Archives Canada Cataloguing in Publication
Weekes Don
        Shootout hockey trivia / Don Weekes

ISBN-13: 978-1-55365-203-8
ISBN-10: 1-55365-203-7
        1. National Hockey League—Miscellanea 2. Hockey—Miscellanea.
I. Title.

GV847.W436 2006   796.962'64   C2006-903225-4

Editing by Anne Rose
Cover and text design by Lisa Hemingway
Cover photo © Jim McIsaac/Getty
Printed and bound in Canada by Friesens
Distributed in the U.S. by Publishers Group West

We gratefully acknowledge the financial support of the Canada Council for the Arts, the British Columbia Arts Council, and the Government of Canada through the Book Publishing Industry Development Program (BPIDP) for our publishing activities.

DON WEEKES *is an award-winning television producer at* CTV *in Montreal. He has written numerous hockey trivia books, including co-authoring the* Unofficial Guide *series.*

Rynewicz

Contents

1

Welcome Back, and a Few Goodbyes

THE IRONY OF BRETT HULL'S just-came-back-to-say-goodbye season of 2005–06 is that, after years of publicly admonishing the NHL for its defense-oriented play, diluted talent and poor marketing, when the league finally revamped its product with rules to increase scoring and speed of play, the Golden Brett was too old to play the NHL's new, exciting game. "Isn't that always the way it goes? The guy who pushes for the changes, who makes the world better, doesn't get to enjoy what he's worked for," said Dallas Stars centre Mike Modano. After 18 NHL seasons, Hull, 41, played just five games for Phoenix post-lockout. Only Wayne Gretzky and Gordie Howe scored more than Hull's 741 career goals.

Answers are on page 8

1.1 **What is the greatest number of NHL games played in one night?**
   A. 12 games
   B. 13 games
   C. 14 games
   D. 15 games

1.2 Which NHL rookie did Wayne Gretzky call "a phenomenal player"—describing one of his goals as "pretty sweet"—in a January 2006 game against the Phoenix Coyotes?

A. Alexander Ovechkin of the Washington Capitals

B. Dion Phaneuf of the Calgary Flames

C. Sidney Crosby of the Pittsburgh Penguins

D. Marek Svatos of the Colorado Avalanche

1.3 In 2005–06, which NHLer claimed to have the blood of a Japanese samurai?

A. Sniper Paul Kariya

B. Tough guy Tie Domi

C. Goalie Jamie Storr

D. Big mouth Jeremy Roenick

1.4 According to Jeremy Roenick, which injury was his most painful?

A. His fractured wrist

B. His shattered jaw

C. His fractured wrist, the second time

D. His broken nose, the eighth time

1.5 Inspired by a Mexican fast food chain, which two NHL general managers actually traded Kari Takko for Rob Bell?

A. Nick Beverly and Mel Bridgman

B. Mike Milbury and Rejean Houle

C. Harry Sinden and Brian Burke

D. Bobby Clarke and Glen Sather

1.6 Which NHL goalie won a wager with his team's captain by eating a live cockroach in 2005–06?

A. Marty Turco of the Dallas Stars

B. Vesa Toskala of the San Jose Sharks

C. Ray Emery of the Ottawa Senators

D. Cristobal Huet of the Montreal Canadiens

1.7 Who is Heavy Eric?

A. The Dallas Stars' equipment manager

B. The mascot of the Ottawa Senators

C. A musician who writes songs about the Vancouver Canucks

D. The Zamboni driver at Chicago's United Center

1.8 The Abby Hoffman Cup is awarded to the women's national champions of the Canadian Amateur Hockey Association. What did Abby Hoffman do to draw international headlines in 1955?

A. She became the youngest athlete at the Olympic winter games

B. To play hockey, she pretended to be a boy

C. She became the first woman to attend an NHL training camp

D. She organizes the World Invitational Tournament for women

1.9 Why did Mike Ricci switch to sweater No. 40 when he joined the San Jose Sharks in 2005–06?

A. To honour a deceased NFL defensive safety

B. It was the lowest number available on the roster

C. As a favour to a family member

D. His usual sweater numbers, 9 and 18, were taken

1.10 **What ended Al MacInnis's NHL career?**

   A. An eye injury

   B. Cartilage damage to his knees

   C. Tendonitis

   D. Stickmakers could no longer produce his preferred hockey sticks

1.11 **Atlanta star Ilya Kovalchuk wears No. 17 on his jersey in honour of which player?**

   A. Soviet forward Alexander Maltsev

   B. Soviet goalie Vladislav Tretiak

   C. Soviet sniper Alexander Yakushev

   D. Soviet superstar Valeri Kharlamov

1.12 **What was the name of the highly publicized 2006 police investigation into a multi-million-dollar sports betting ring involving prominent NHLers?**

   A. Investigation Penalty Box

   B. Operation Slap Shot

   C. Investigation Face Off

   D. Operation Betzky

1.13 **What event made Dean Mayrand newsworthy in 2005?**

   A. The trial over a failed murder plot to kill a hockey agent

   B. The players' lockout of 2004–05

   C. The Battle of the Hockey Enforcers slugfest

   D. An impaired driving charge after the death of a prominent athlete

1.14 **What was the so-called "Shanahan Summit"?**

A. Brendan Shanahan's personal top 10 list of NHL snipers

B. A team of All-Stars barnstorming during the 2004–05 lockout

C. A nickname for the 2005 World Junior Championships

D. A meeting between hockey personalities to make the game more exciting

1.15 **During the lockout of 2004–05, who produced the "Bring It Back" TV commercials featuring abandoned 19,000-seat arenas and melting ice?**

A. Molson

B. General Motors

C. Nike Canada

D. The NHL Players Association

1.16 **Who scored the most shootout goals in 2005–06?**

A. Sergei Zubov of the Dallas Stars

B. Miroslav Satan of the New York Islanders

C. Jussi Jokinen of the Dallas Stars

D. Viktor Kozlov of the New Jersey Devils

1.17 **Under the new NHL rules adopted in 2005–06 governing shootouts, who is credited with the game-winning goal in a shootout win?**

A. No one is credited

B. The first player to score in the shootout

C. The last player to score in the shootout

D. All players from the winning team who scored

1.18 How many more faceoffs did Rod Brind'Amour take than any other player in 2005–06?

A. Less than 100 faceoffs

B. Between 100 and 200 faceoffs

C. Between 200 and 300 faceoffs

D. More than 300 faceoffs

1.19 What was the salary difference between San Jose's Joe Thornton and Jonathan Cheechoo when they became line-mates in 2005–06?

A. Less than U.S.$1 million

B. Between U.S.$1 and U.S.$3 million

C. Between U.S.$3 and U.S.$5 million

D. More than U.S.$5 million

1.20 In terms of ice time, which player earning a minimum of U.S.$450,000 delivered best bang for the buck for his team in 2005–06?

A. Jamie Heward of the Washington Capitals

B. Jarred Smithson of the Nashville Predators

C. Cristobal Huet of the Montreal Canadiens

D. Mark Hartigan of the Columbus Blue Jackets

1.21 What was Jaromir Jagr referring to in 2005–06 when he said, "I'll bet all my money they're legal"?

A. His pre-game meds

B. His elbow pads

C. His hockey sticks

D. His goaltender's leg pads

1.22 Which NHL player launched his own entertainment company and hip-hop record label in 2005?

A. Jeremy Roenick
B. Anson Carter
C. Jarome Iginla
D. José Théodore

1.23 Who did Florida sniper Olli Jokinen credit for rescuing his NHL career after signing a multi-year contract with the Panthers in 2005–06?

A. European scout Niklas Blomgren
B. General Manager Mike Keenan
C. Coach Jacques Martin
D. Veteran Joe Nieuwendyk

1.24 On March 3, 2006, the night Pat LaFontaine's number was retired in Buffalo, which Toronto Maple Leaf was playing in his 1,000th NHL game against the Sabres?

A. Tie Domi
B. Eric Lindros
C. Mats Sundin
D. Ed Belfour

1.25 Which NHLer made headlines when his likeness was inaccurately produced as an action figure in 2004?

A. Jarome Iginla
B. Donald Brashear
C. Kevin Weekes
D. Anson Carter

Answers

1.1   **D. 15 games**
The NHL's strategy after emerging from the lockout that
wiped out 2004–05 was a season-opening night unlike any
other in the league's 87-year history. Several story lines
dominated the headlines, including the Lightning finally
raising its Stanley Cup banner in Tampa Bay; Wayne Gretzky's
coaching debut; the first game of 18-year-old phenom Sidney
Crosby; many new rules to crack down on fouls, and the first
ever shootout. To bring the fans back, ticket prices were also
slashed overall by 7.5 per cent, two-thirds of NHL clubs cut
ticket costs and all 30 teams were in action on the same night
for the first time since 1928–29, when the league had 10 teams.
The 15-game total eclipsed the previous mark of 14, which had
been done nine times. A record 275,447 fans showed up for
the comeback celebration on October 5, 2005.

1.2   **A. Alexander Ovechkin of the Washington Capitals**
Wayne Gretzky knows something about greatness, so when
he praises a player his comments reverberate throughout
the hockey world. "You know, he's a phenomenal player and
he's been a tremendous influence in the game," said Gretzky
after his Phoenix Coyotes were whipped 6–1 by the Capitals
in January 2006. The Great One was talking about Ovechkin's
two-goal, three-point contribution in the win and, more
specifically, the effort he made on the goal "that was pretty
sweet." After being sent sprawling by a hit from Coyotes

defenseman Paul Mara, the 20-year-old Russian slid past goalie Brian Boucher towards the corner boards, rolled from his back to his chest and tapped the puck with his stick blade in a blindsided effort to score from a near-impossible angle. The puck whipped past a startled Boucher, who had given up on the play. "I saw the net, then I saw the puck, but not at the same moment. I shot the puck without really knowing where the net or I was," said Ovechkin of what many have called the greatest goal of 2005–06.

1.3 C. Goalie Jamie Storr

Few NHLers are of Asian heritage, with Paul Kariya being the most famous. Less well-known is Philadelphia's Jamie Storr, who doesn't look part-Asian (like Kariya)—until he dons his mask, which is decorated with his mother's initials and Japan's Rising Sun on the back, fiery dragons on the side and, leaving no mistake as to his identity, his name written in Japanese on the front. But the mask and its oriental motif are just part of Storr's warrior arsenal. He claims to also have the blood of Japan's most famous soldiers in his veins. "I have been told that my mother's grandfather was a samurai, so I have the blood of a samurai," says Storr. Storr's mother and father met in Brampton, Ontario, in 1967. His mother, Keiko, was born December 7, 1941—the day Japan bombed Pearl Harbour.

1.4 B. His shattered jaw

In the August 2004 edition of *Esquire* magazine, readers were treated to several amazing first-person accounts in an article called "What it Feels Like." The experiences ranged from what many would call insane (catching a great white shark), to the terrifying (surviving a tsunami), to the absurd (staying awake for 11 days). But Jeremy Roenick also got some ink with what it feels like "... to shatter your jaw," his most painful injury "by far," which he suffered in February 2004 as he played against the New York Rangers at MSG. In his *Esquire* account of the incident, Roenick detailed the gruesome facts better than any play-by-play announcer. Here's a sample: "I was on the ice, my face in a pool of blood. When I came to I felt like somebody was standing on the side of my face, stomping on it. When I went to bite down, my teeth didn't line up... There were pieces of bone, of jaw, moving around, and I almost fainted... There was actually a perfect broken-bone imprint of the puck in my jaw." Roenick played again in six weeks—the bare minimum "wait time."

1.5 D. Bobby Clarke and Glen Sather

We have always suspected that Bobby Clarke and Glen Sather have evil minds. Now here's more proof. In November 1990, Clarke, who was then general manager of the Minnesota North Stars, and Sather, then general manager of the Edmonton Oilers, engineered a player trade that appears to have been made merely to satisfy both men's warped sense of humour. Clarke sent backup goalie Kari Takko to the Oilers in return for defenseman Bruce Bell, thus completing the first and only Takko-Bell deal. Only Bell had an NHL career, and played just one more game—for the Oilers.

1.6 C. Ray Emery of the Ottawa Senators

His teammates already knew Ray Emery was a different kind of character, but just how different became clear when the Senators goalkeeper accepted a $500 bet from captain Daniel

Alfredsson to gobble a cockroach that had scuttled across the floor of the team's dressing room during an October 2005 game against the Carolina Hurricanes. "I'd crush on *Fear Factor*," said Emery, who used the $500 reward to obtain an elaboate new tattoo on his right arm that read "Anger Is a Gift." The choice of tattoo probably didn't sit well with Ottawa's coaching staff, which had ordered Emery to take an anger management course.

1.7 **C. A musician who writes songs about the Vancouver Canucks**

Known in Vancouver music circles as Heavy Eric (with or without his band, the Light Weights), Eric Holmquist has been writing and recording songs about the Vancouver Canucks for more than a decade. The former lumberjack, part-time Elvis impersonator and full-time mailman has had his music featured on Vancouver radio and TV shows—and at GM Place. Heavy Eric's first hockey hymn, "Gino, Gino," penned in 1991, paid tribute to enforcer Gino Odjick. Since then, Holmquist has written 20 more ditties about his beloved Canucks, including two that focus on the team's controversial No. 44: "They've Freed Todd Bertuzzi" and "It's Called the Todd Bertuzzi" (a tune that can be downloaded as a ring tone for cellphones). However, Heavy Eric is still waiting to write the song that will crown his music career—the one about his favourite team winning the Stanley Cup.

1.8 **B. To play hockey, she pretended to be a boy**

Women and hockey date back to the 1890s, when college women first played the game at McGill University in Montreal. Leagues were organized soon after, and one team, the Preston

Rivulettes from Ontario, were the Canadian champions for 10 years during the 1930s. But no player generated more interest in women in hockey than eight-year-old Abby Hoffman, a Toronto girl who cut her hair short just so she could play hockey in the only league available during the 1950s—a boys' league. Hoffman proved as good an actor as hockey player. Her secret was discovered only after she produced her birth certificate (which was necessary for playing on the Toronto Hockey League's All-Star team). Subsequently dismissed from the team, Hoffman made headlines around the world. Today, Abby Hoffman is still a noted Canadian sports figure.

1.9   **A. To honour a deceased NFL defensive safety**
During his 15-year NHL career, Mike Ricci only ever wore No. 9 or 18 on his back, but after hearing about Pat Tillman, he switched to No. 40. Tillman, a four-year veteran with the NFL Arizona Cardinals, turned down a lucrative U.S. $3.6-million contract in 2002 to enlist with the U.S. Army Rangers in the wake of the terrorist attacks in New York on September 11, 2001. But after joining up with Operation Mountain Storm to fight Al-Queda in Afghanistan, Tillman's battalion came under enemy fire in a roadside ambush, and Tillman was killed in action. "My great grandfather was at Pearl Harbour and a lot of my family has gone and fought in wars, and I really haven't done a damn thing as far as laying myself on the line like that," Tillman had told NBC News after 9/11. He was the first NFLer killed in combat since Buffalo tackle Bob Kalsu died in the Vietnam War in July 1970. "When I heard the story, it really touched me," said Ricci. "This is a way to pay tribute to what he did." Tillman wore No. 40 with the Cardinals.

1.10 A. An eye injury

A lot of shot-blockers and goalies drew a collective sigh of relief in September 2005, when Al MacInnis retired his fearsome slap shot. No longer would they face the Shot, the 100-m.p.h. (161 km/h) howitzer responsible for many of the 1,274 points MacInnis scored during his illustrious 22-year career. Indeed, when he joined the NHL in the early 1980s, MacInnis had *only* the Shot in his toolbox. "When he broke in with us, he was a one-dimensional player," says Cliff Fletcher, former Calgary GM. "He could shoot the puck and do it better than anybody. But he wasn't a great defenseman. He had trouble turning, he wasn't strong and his skating had to be improved." But MacInnis worked hard at making himself a complete player—as hard as he'd needed to to hone his superior shooting skills while growing up, firing buckets of pucks against the family barn in Port Hood, Nova Scotia. "A lot of guys shoot hard," says Paul Coffey, "but nobody ever scattered on Al's teams when he was shooting. He *knew* where the puck was going." A seven-time All-Star who played in 12 All-Star games, MacInnis won the NHL's hardest-shot competitions more than any player in history. MacInnis ended his career after successive eye injuries permanently damaged his peripheral vision in 2001 and 2003.

1.11 D. Soviet superstar Valeri Kharlamov

Even though Ilya Kovalchuk was born two years after Kharlamov's death in 1981, the Atlanta sniper still wears No. 17 in memory of Kharlamov. The late Soviet hockey star was considered among the best Russian forwards on the Soviet team that played Team Canada in the historic Summit Series of 1972. In fact, he was so highly regarded by the Canadian players that, in Game 6, Bobby Clarke paid him the ultimate compliment: a two-hand slash that broke the Soviet's ankle. Kharlamov missed Game 7 and played injured in Game 8; the Soviets lost both games and the series. Although Kharlamov never set any scoring records, his inventive play and virtuosity with the puck in bypassing defensemen was pure wizardry. Racing down the ice, his body would be a blur as he wove and deked to fake out the opposition—a style of play that would be studied and adopted by the next generation of superstars, including Wayne Gretzky and Igor Larionov. In another tribute to Kharlamov, each year the Soviet newspaper *Sovetsky Sport* awards Russia's top NHLer the Kharlamov Trophy. Nominated by his fellow Russian NHLers, the winner in 2003–04 was Kovalchuk, who received 58 out of 63 votes. It was an honour truly befitting Atlanta's No. 17.

1.12 B. Operation Slap Shot

Gambling on professional sporting events is nothing new, but when players themselves are betting, or, as in this case, allegedly running the books, things get dicey. After a three-month police probe (dubbed Operation Slap Shot by the New Jersey State Police), investigators announced they had uncovered an illegal gambling operation financed by Phoenix Coyote assistant coach Rick Tocchet and tied to the Bruno-Scarfo organized crime family in Philadelphia and New Jersey. So what prominent NHL figures allegedly placed bets through the ring? Wayne Gretzky's wife, Janet. During a 40-day period between December 29, 2005, and February 5, 2006, police said the betting operation processed more than 1,000 wagers, totalling U.S.$1.7 million, on mostly football and basketball games.

1.13 **C. The Battle of the Hockey Enforcers slugfest**
The idea didn't even look good on paper, but promoters
of a night of fights on ice weren't deterred. Despite much
opposition by hockey purists and anti-violence supporters,
two years of searching for a city to host the event and being
booted out of Minneapolis, banned in Winnipeg and cancelled in Prince George, B.C., the threat of a lawsuit finally
brought the Battle of the Hockey Enforcers to the spectators
and pay-per-view airwaves. Yet only some 2,000 fans finally
watched the slugfest live at the Prince George Multiplex in
August 2005, when Dean Mayrand of the Mission Sorel-Tracy
of Quebec's North American Professional Hockey League
picked up $62,000 for beating up AHL Syracuse Crunch for-
ward Mike Sgroi in the final round. The most familiar name
on the card was former NHLer Link Gaetz, who withdrew
after his first fight.

1.14 **D. A meeting between hockey personalities to make the
game more exciting**
NHL fans knew the league had finally got it right after wit-
nessing the first night of hockey in 2005–06. In Nashville's
opener, Steve Sullivan took the puck in San Jose's corner,
faked out Sharks winger Marco Sturm and turned defenseman Tom Preissing into a pretzel before sliding a pass to
winger Scott Walker at the far post for a tap-in. Sullivan later
said that, a few years earlier, he would have been sticked
between the legs and pinned against the glass after his
second move—exactly the kind of clutch-and-grab hockey
Brendan Shanahan was trying to eliminate when he organized a two-day conference of players, coaches, GMs, on-ice
officials and media in December 2004. Shanahan's credibility

as a veteran scorer, tough guy and Cup-winner made him the perfect player to pull together such a diverse group to share ideas on how to open up the game and make hockey fun again, as with Sullivan's "dipsy-dos" on the tap-in goal by Walker. Shanahan wasn't solely responsible for the crackdown on interference or the other rule changes that tweaked the game in 2005–06, but his summit established the NHL competition committee that was the first step in injecting more entertainment into the game.

1.15 C. Nike Canada

During the NHL lockout, the Canadian airwaves were saturated with commercials lamenting the lack of hockey, such as Molson Canadian's 30-second montage of weepy fans singing the 1980s Culture Club hit "Do You Really Want to Hurt Me?" in the beer-maker's "Hockey, Please Come Back" campaign. But Nike made a more forceful appeal to Canadians and their collective passion for hockey with its simple "Bring it Back" spot, which featured the stark image of a vacant arena interior—silent except for the crackle of melting ice.

1.16 C. Jussi Jokinen of the Dallas Stars

Without question, the most anticipated rule change in 2005–06 was the introduction of the shootout. The controversial one-on-one tiebreaker had fans standing in their seats and many condemning it as anti-team and, even, unhockeylike. Sure. Meanwhile, little-known Jussi Jokinen turned goalies inside out and converted a perfect nine of nine shootouts, until late season, when on March 18 he missed the net on his 10th attempt against San Jose's Vesa Toskala. Jokinen was merely mortal after that, finishing the year with a league-high 10 shootout goals on 13 tries for a stellar 76.9 shoot-percentage, the highest of any player with six or more attempts. The Oilers' Ales Hemsky led all shooters with 14 tries, but scored only five times, for a 35.7 per cent. Surprisingly, the worst shooter was Colorado sniper Joe Sakic, who was held scoreless on seven attempts.

1.17   A. No one is credited

Shootout goals and goals-against are not credited in individual statistics. According to Rule 89b, Note 6, the player who scores the game-winner in a shootout does not receive credit for the goal in his personal stats, and the losing goalkeeper is not charged with the extra goal-against. Regardless of the number of goals scored during the shootout, the final score is always one more goal that its opponent, based on the score at the end of overtime. The visiting team shoots first. In 2005–06, there were 330 goals on 981 attempts, with goalies stopping two of every three shots. Edmonton played a league-high 16 games, going 7–9; Dallas netted the most shootout wins, with a 12–1 record.

1.18   D. More than 300 faceoffs

There's not much that Rod Brind'Amour didn't do for Carolina in 2005–06—or, for that matter, any team the two-way centre has played for in his 16-year career. That's because Brind'Amour never takes a game off. As well, versatility is his trademark, from scoring goals to blocking shots. At age 35, he led all forwards in ice time with an average of 24:29 per game. And those numbers were usually earned against the other team's top line, including penalty kills and faceoffs, which Brind'Amour did 2,145 times—winning 1,267, almost 350 more faceoffs than any NHLer—for a winning-percentage of 59.11 in 2005–06. He was also the Hurricanes' triggerman on 44 per cent of their draws, besting rival Joe Thornton, who had 37 per cent of San Jose's faceoffs. (The NHL has been keeping statistics on faceoffs since 1997–98.)

1.19 **D. More than U.S.$5 million**

No matter how good a tandem looks on paper, teaming your best shooter and playmaker isn't always successful. In fact, finding the right chemistry between players usually happens by accident, because a great scoring duo that naturally feeds off each other demands a skill set that can't be practised or taught. Which is why San Jose's blockbuster trade for Joe Thornton in November 2005 and his subsequent pairing with Jonathan Cheechoo proved more a stroke of luck than genius. In theory, superstar centre Thornton would be double-teamed, providing more space for Cheechoo to score, while Thornton, a left-shooting centre, would complement Cheechoo's right shot. In reality, the pair clicked from the start. While Thornton drew the fire, he could still make seam passes into quiet areas that Cheechoo skated into to get an open shot and finish the play. It gave the Sharks the league's most lethal twosome and turned Cheechoo into a bona fide sniper. The pair captured NHL trophies as point and goal leaders, with Thornton amassing a league-high 125 points and Cheechoo besting all scorers with 56 goals (Thornton assisted on 38 of them). But salary-wise, the two couldn't be much further apart. When they became linemates, Thornton was earning U.S.$6.66 million and Cheechoo, U.S.$760,000—a U.S.$5.9-million difference. Late in 2005–06, Cheechoo signed a five-year U.S.$15-million contract extension. Good thinking.

1.20 **A. Jamie Heward of the Washington Capitals**

Among minimum-salary players in 2005–2006, Jamie Heward
more than proved his value for Washington. After spots in
four NHL cities and three Swiss clubs, the U.S.$450,000-defen-
seman led the Capitals with 21.51 minutes per game, ranked
22nd in the NHL with 29.0 shifts per game, recorded 140 shots
on goal and blocked more than 100. He also recorded seven
goals on 28 points—a career high. But Cristobal Huet was
a strong challenger. The Montreal goalie earned just above
minimum compensation, U.S.$456,000, and led the league
with a .929 save-percentage in 36 games as well as taking the
Canadiens to a playoff spot after a seventh-place finish in the
Eastern Conference.

1.21 **C. His hockey sticks**

After making headlines in 2004 for an on-line gambling
habit that drained him of a reputed U.S.$500,000, Jaromir
Jagr should probably think twice about further references
to betting—or to using illegal sticks. His bravado may have
cost the Rangers two points and a win in their March 8, 2006,
game against Atlanta. Referee Don Koharski, who nailed
Jagr twice for using an illegal stick, penalized him during
overtime and then disqualified him in the shootout in the
3–2 loss to the Thrashers. Asked if the illegal-stick call felled
the Rangers, New York coach Tom Renney said, "Jag's a pretty
good scorer. He had a better than 50–50 chance of scoring, so
yeah, maybe." But it was not Jagr's first offense for playing
with a banned blade. In a November 26, 2005, game against
Washington, after the Capitals called for a measurement,
the five-time scoring champion was nabbed with a prohibited
stick at the start of overtime. After the game, Caps goalie

Olie Kolzig said, "We played with him for three years so we all knew." After the Olympic break in 2006, the NHL instituted a rule requiring that all players involved in shootouts must have their sticks measured. As well, sticks may not be curved more than half an inch (1.27 cm).

1.22   B. Anson Carter

Anson Carter, one of the few black hockey players in the NHL, isn't shy about his love of hip-hop. During the 2005 NHL lock-out, the dreadlocked Vancouver Canucks winger launched his own record label, Big Up Entertainment. "As of right now, we are building the ground level to be a multi-faceted entertainment company," Carter told AllHipHop.com. The first release from the independent label was the single "Passion and Pain," by Main & Merc of Richmond, Virginia. And while that pair worked on their debut album, Carter announced plans to turn Big Up into a full-blown media company, with sports, music and fashion divisions. The company's first film, *Bald,* a comedy similar to *American Pie,* is about a college student struggling to prevent his hair from falling out.

1.23   B. General Manager Mike Keenan

Iron Mike was notorious for his motivational strategies. And though his hard-line approach failed to inspire several notable underachievers, many of his whipping boys matured under his demanding tutelage. Still, Keenan's whine mellowed with age. With the Panthers, his seventh team, he used his new, softer approach to rejuvenate the career of Olli Jokinen, a fading prospect who was on his third club in four years. Keenan gave Jokinen more ice time and named him captain. The Finn responded stat-wise and at the 2006 trading deadline showed that his loyalty went beyond big money. "Before Mike came here I was playing fourth line," Jokinen said in a *National Post* story. "… he really pushed me hard and gave me all kinds of chances to play, and I proved what kind of player I am." Jokinen's new contract was a four-year U.S.$21-million deal.

1.24 A. Tie Domi

Few thought Tie Domi would ever achieve the 1,000-game milestone. The odds of long-term NHL success usually run against any player with a fists-first philosophy. But Domi proved to be more than tough, matching his pugilistic skills with a tireless work ethic and hard-driving ambition that kept him in a Maple Leaf uniform longer than any teammate except Mats Sundin. It's a notable achievement considering Domi only scored his 100th goal in October 2005, almost 15 years after his first. Still, the fourth-line winger with 3,515 career penalty minutes couldn't inspire Toronto. They were outclassed 6–2 in Domi's 1,000th game against Buffalo, a team celebrating its own past beneath the freshly hung banner of Pat LaFontaine's No. 16.

1.25 A. Jarome Iginla

When the three-inch (7.6-cm) Jarome Iginla figure rolled off the production line in 2004, officials with McFarlane Toys, the liscensed manufacturers of NHL figures, had to be a little red-faced. In the two-pack set containing a miniature likeness of Ignila and Saku Koivu, the Iginla figure had the lighter skin pigmentation of the two players. Beacause of a mistake made in the skin-wash process, the fair-skinned Koivu had a deep suntan and Iginla was as pale as his real-life Nordic counterpart. But this was good news for sports memorabilia collectors, who see a spike in demand for collectibles with even the tiniest imperfections.

The Third Jersey

MORE THAN JUST SUPPLYING additional income, the third jersey gave a completely new look to the league's more traditionally dressed clubs. Some teams hit the mark with their alternate logos and sweater designs, but others struck out, including the Dallas Stars, who, after making about U.S.$400,000, mothballed their incredibly unpopular third jersey in April 2006. In this game, match the teams in the left column with their third-jersey designs.

Solutions are on page 119

1. _____NYR   A. Brown bear

2. _____Calgary   B. Sabre-tooth tiger protruding out of a triangle

3. _____Columbus   C. Replica of a 1938 jersey

4. _____Ottawa   D. Bull's head with a star constellation

5. _____Edmonton   E. The *Statue of Liberty*'s head

6. _____Los Angeles F. Horse head snorting fire

7. _____Montreal   G. Replica of a 1945 jersey

8. _____Nashville   H. Coat of arms

9. _____Boston   I. Drop of oil in a gear-like design

10._____Dallas   J. A Roman's head, looking out

11._____Toronto   K. A star, wrapped in the Ohio State flag

2

The *H*oly Goalie and
Other *S*aviours

THE GAME HAD 15 GOALS, 14 power plays and four lead changes, but when it was finally over, Ed Belfour had secured his place in history by notching his 448th career-win in the 9–6 victory against the New York Islanders, December 19, 2005. It took the 40-year-old goalie six tries in a three-week span after tying the great Terry Sawchuk with win number 447 on November 28. "It took forever," said Belfour. "The guys just played unbelievable. It took nine goals, but I'm really thankful and honoured." Belfour trails only Patrick Roy's 551 wins on the all-time list.

Answers are on page 27

2.1 **Who was the Holy Goalie?**
- A. Joe Daley, the WHA's all-time career leader in wins
- B. John Garrett, the WHA's all-time career leader in losses
- C. Ernie Wakely, the WHA's all-time career leader in minutes played
- D. Ron Grahame, the WHA's all-time career leader in goals-against

2.2 How many victories did it take to establish Ottawa goalie Ray Emery's record for most consecutive wins from the start of a career?

A. Five consecutive wins

B. Seven consecutive wins

C. Nine consecutive wins

D. 11 consecutive wins

2.3 What was the most shootout wins recorded by a goalie in 2005–06?

A. Seven shootout wins

B. Eight shootout wins

C. Nine shootout wins

D. 10 shootout wins

2.4 How many rounds was the longest shootout in 2005–06?

A. Five rounds

B. 10 rounds

C. 15 rounds

D. 20 rounds

2.5 In 2005–06, which NHL goalie donned a mask with the painted image of a gangster holding a gun and smoking a cigar?

A. Nikolai Khabibulin of the Chicago Blackhawks

B. Mathieu Garon of the Los Angeles Kings

C. Manny Legace of the Detroit Red Wings

D. Antero Niittymaki of the Philadelphia Flyers

2.6 Which goalie did Mark Messier victimize the most?

A. Ron Hextall

B. Tom Barrasso

C. Brian Hayward

D. Richard Brodeur

2.7 **Why was Hall of Fame defenseman Lionel Conacher called the Travelling Netminder?**

A. He was a goalie coach for several clubs

B. After hockey, he was a travelling salesman

C. His unique shot-blocking style

D. He subbed for many teams before the two-goalie system

2.8 **What medical ailment caused goalie Jeff Hackett to retire in February 2004?**

A. Ulcers

B. Diabetes

C. Vertigo

D. Muscular dystrophy

2.9 **How many consecutive games did Buffalo's Martin Biron win after switching his brand of goalie stick in 2005-06?**

A. Four games in a row

B. Seven games in a row

C. 10 games in a row

D. 13 games in a row

2.10 **What was so unusual about goalie Dan Blackburn's style of play?**

A. He wore two left skates

B. He was ambidextrous

C. He rarely went down, because of a back ailment

D. He played wearing two blockers

2.11 When goalies Ken and Dave Dryden were growing up, which little-known netminder did they idolize?

A. New York's Joe Schaeffer

B. Detroit's Julian Klymkiw

C. Montreal's Hal Murphy

D. Chicago's Moe Roberts

2.12 In what decade was the first modern-day goalie pad invented?

A. The 1910s

B. The 1920s

C. The 1930s

D. The 1940s

2.13 What NHL first did rookie goalie James Howard of Detroit accomplish in his first two career games in 2005–06?

A. He received two fighting majors

B. He faced two penalty shots

C. He earned assists in both games

D. He recorded two shootouts

2.14 At a 2006 auction of Jacques Plante memorabilia, who made the highest bid for Plante's 1960s-era goalie mask?

A. Jacques Plante's family

B. Goalie José Théodore

C. A Canadian museum

D. The Hockey Hall of Fame

2.15 As of the 2006 playoffs, which goalie recorded the most regular-season games without a playoff appearance?

A. Martin Biron

B. Roberto Luongo

C. Mike Dunham

D. Dunc Wilson

2.16 **As of 2005–06, who was the last Toronto goalie to blank the New York Rangers in regular-season play?**

A. Johnny Bower

B. Felix Potvin

C. Curtis Joseph

D. Ed Belfour

2.17 **What is the record for most victories by a netminder in one month?**

A. Eight wins

B. 10 wins

C. 12 wins

D. 14 wins

The Holy Goalie and Other Saviours

Answers

2.1 **A. Joe Daley, the WHA's all-time career leader in wins**

Joe Daley played 105 NHL games, but is best remembered for the second stage of his career as an original member of the Winnipeg Jets. Daley joined the club in 1972, during the formation of the World Hockey Association, and stayed until the league folded in 1979—one of only five players to have played every season of the WHA's existence with the same team. Some say Daley was a religious man, and to Winnipeggers he was widely known as the Holy Goalie. Certainly, the Jets were saviours to a city starved for professional play. Daley answered their prayers, backstopping the Jets to three Avco Cup championships. When the WHA merged with the NHL, Daley retired as the netminder with the most wins in league history.

2.2   C. Nine consecutive wins

It took Ray Emery four years, but the Ottawa rookie isn't complaining, considering his real estate in the record books. Emery went 6–0 in early 2005–06 to erase Philadelphia's Bob Froese record of eight straight wins from a career start. Emery's other three victories date back four seasons, when he was 1–0–0 as backup to Patrick Lalime in 2002–03 and 2–0–0 for his second and third career wins in 2003–04. Emery capped the record with his first NHL shutout, a 4–0 whitewash versus Montreal on November 29, 2005.

2.3   B. Eight shootout wins

During the first shootout season, three goalies shared the lead with eight wins: Dallas' Marty Turco, Martin Brodeur of New Jersey and the Islanders' Rick Dipietro. Brodeur and DiPietro, who played in a league-high 11 games, each had three losses; Turco registered only one. DiPietro faced the most shots (41) and Brodeur had the best save-percentage (.763) of the three. Washington's Olaf Kolzig, with four wins and five losses, had 44 shots-against in one-on-one play, the most among all netminders. But the season's big surprise was star netminder Miikka Kiprusoff of Calgary, who netted only one win in eight shootout games and allowed 12 goals on 23 shots. It was the worst save-percentage (.478) among goalies with at least one shootout victory in 2005–06.

2.4   C. 15 rounds

During its first season featuring the shootout format to determine the outcome of tied games, the NHL recorded 145 matches involving shootouts, though none longer than the marathon 15-round duelling match between the New York Rangers and Washington Capitals on November 26. Based on the new rules, if the score remains tied after each team has taken three shots, the shootout proceeds to a sudden-death format with each team shooting once in successive rounds. A winner is declared only when one team scores in the round. In the New York–Washington game, rookie netminder Henrik Lundqvist went head-to-head against counterpart Olie Kolzig as the Rangers' Michael Nylander, Ville Nieminen and Jason Strudwick all scored to keep the shootout going, with Nylander matching the Capitals' Andrew Cassels goal in the second round, Nieminen equalling Brian Willsie's sixth-round score and Strudwick countering Bryan Muir's 14th-round goal. Then, in the 15th round, after the Caps' Matt Bradley wrist shot failed, defenseman Marek Malik fooled Kolzig on a trick shot with his stick between his skates. "I was watching everything before me," said Malik, the third-to-last shooter available on the Ranger bench. "Olie was unbelievable. He stopped everything, from shots, moves. I just thought to myself, 'Maybe I'll surprise him.' I tried the move and it worked." It was Malik's first goal of the regular season. "You have to have guts to do that move," said Jaromir Jagr. "In front of 20,000 people watching you, it's not that easy to do." The trick goal ended the NHL's longest shootout in the 15th round to give New York a 3–2 win over Washington. "It was actually kind of fun," said loser Kolzig to the Associated Press. "On this stage, Madison Square Garden, Saturday night… I didn't expect Malik to pull off a move like that."

2.5 D. Antero Niittymaki of the Philadelphia Flyers

When Antero Niittymaki played in Finland, his nickname was Antsu, but during his short NHL stint in February 2004, Flyers coach Ken Hitchcock started calling Niittymaki "Frank," after the infamous Prohibition-era mobster Frank Nitti. Once Niittymaki understood what the nickname meant, he had his mask repainted with a gangster theme. The design depicts Frank Nitti smoking a cigar and holding a gun, with smoking bullets below. Said Hitchcock: "I guess I was the first to call him that. I never thought in my wildest dreams he would go and put it on his bloody mask."

2.6 D. Richard Brodeur

Vancouver fans nicknamed Brodeur "King Richard," due to his sometimes dazzling play. The goalie ruled for eight years as the Canucks' number one backstopper and carried them all the way to the stunning Stanley Cup finals of 1982. Brodeur's reign also overlapped Mark Messier's most prolific scoring period, but even though Messier continued to play for 16 years *after* Brodeur retired, King Richard still holds the title as Messier's court jester. Brodeur gave up an all-time-high 20 goals to the Moose, followed by Ron Hextall's 16.

2.7 C. His unique shot-blocking style

Lionel Conacher will forever be known as Big Train and Canada's athlete of the half-century, but he also earned the nickname the Travelling Netminder for his distinctive shot-blocking technique. In a calculated attempt to dissuade opponents from shooting, Conacher would slide across the ice on one knee with his gloves open-palmed to block the puck. The move allowed Conacher to stay upright without being vulnerable to a fake shot or deke, while at the same time cutting down the angle on the net. It forced the shooter into a quick decision, such as turning over the puck with a flawed offensive move.

2.8   C. Vertigo

As hockey ailments go, this one was definitely unusual. In January 2004, Hackett was diagnosed with positional vertigo, described as "a false sensation of motion or spinning that leads to dizziness and discomfort." The condition, which was triggered by an inner-ear infection, afflicted Hackett after he tended net for the Philadelphia Flyers on January 13, 2004. "It happened later that night," said Hackett. "I went to bed and everything was spinning. When I got up, I kept falling to my right, catching myself just in time. It was the same in the morning." After spending a month on the sidelines with little improvement, the 15-year veteran announced his retirement.

2.9   D. 13 games in a row

Martin Biron is no hockey pitchman—until it comes to talking about his Montreal-brand goalie paddle. And why shouldn't he be effusive about the Finnish hockey equipment manufacturer? After the Sabres goalie switched to Montreal's composite shaft with wooden paddle and blade in early November 2005, he went on a 13-game tear between November 15 and December 17. Not that Biron wasn't happy with his Koho/ccm sticks; he just got a little bored waiting for a start as backup to number one man Ryan Miller. That boredom got Biron talking to Buffalo defenseman Teppo Numminen, the owner, product tester and player representative of Montreal Sports in the North American market. Biron got his new sticks almost at the same time as Miller went down with a broken right thumb, a lucky break for Biron.

The Sabres gelled and Biron earned the longest streak by an NHL goalie since Detroit's Chris Osgood won the same number in 1995–96. During that stretch, Buffalo won nine road games, almost equalling its own NHL record of 10, set in 1983–84.

2.10 D. He played wearing two blockers

For all the media and fan attention Dan Blackburn received when he became the third-youngest netminder to win an NHL game in 2001–02, you'd think he was the next Patrick Roy. But four years later, the 23-year-old netminder was back-stopping the minor league Victoria Salmon Kings—by most standards, your basic career malfunction after being picked 10th overall in 2001, followed by a 63-game stint with the New York Rangers. The reason for all the media hype was Blackburn's blocker-catcher hybrid glove. He wore it in place of a typical trapper, which was useless to Blackburn after a freak injury to his left shoulder left him with permanent nerve damage that prevented him from rotating his hand into an upright catching position. Playing with the Salmon Kings, Blackburn adapted to a more positional game to compensate for the hitch in his glove game. But it did little to help his return, and, in September 2005, Blackburn officially retired. He is the only modern-day goaltender to play wearing two blockers.

2.11 B. Detroit's Julian Klymkiw

Julian who? Klymkiw was Detroit's assistant trainer and practice goalie when the Drydens were growing up in the late 1950s. He played only one NHL game, but starred in *Shootout in the NHL*, a CBS between-periods feature. Klymkiw, who zeroed all the top guns of the day, unknowingly became a fan favourite of Ken and Dave, who used to fight over who would pretend to be him. Klymkiw's one real game came in 1958, playing not for his Red Wings but the New York Rangers. With only one goalie per team, all clubs in that era had a substitute netminder available at home games in case of injury to either team's regular goalie. So when New York's Gump Worsley pulled a tendon during the Red Wings' home opener, Klymkiw stepped between the pipes—for the opposition. It might have been the pressure of playing against his own team, but Klymkiw didn't perform nearly as well as on *Shootout in the NHL*, giving up two goals during his 19 minutes of fame. Detroit won 3–0 and Klymkiw never played in the NHL again. Still, he faced more NHL stars on breakaways than any other one-game goalie.

2.12   B. The 1920s

Emil "Pop" Kenesky is generally credited with inventing, in 1924, the first quasi-modern goalie leg pads. Kenesky was working as a harness-maker in Hamilton, Ontario, when Jake Forbes, an NHL goalie for the Hamilton Tigers, asked him to repair the cricket pads he had been using. The result was an unusual combination of horse hide, felt and rubberized canvas, with kapok for stuffing in the front and deer hair on the sides. Kenesky's big, thick, leather pads ended a long losing streak for Forbes, and the Hamilton craftsman soon became the pad-maker of choice for goaltending's elite. His handiwork (and later that of his son, Jack) protected the legs of every top netminder during the six-team era and beyond, including Tony Esposito's and Ken Dryden's. Kenesky's pad design underwent very few changes, the shape staying essentially the same for five decades—with the exception of an added scoop at the pad's base for shock absorption and

padding that fit around either side of the skate. But during
the 1990s, hockey's first family of goalie pads finally closed
up shop, unable to compete as old-world tradesmen in a high-
tech age of lighter and more water-resistant materials.

2.13 B. He faced two penalty shots

A few goalies in NHL history have faced back-to-back penalty
shots in consecutive games, and, in one case, two in one game.
But in an NHL first of its kind for a rookie, James Howard faced
penalty shots in his first two career starts. In his NHL debut
against Los Angeles on November 28, 2005, Howard gave up a
goal to Joe Corvo on a penalty shot in a 5–2 win. Then, in his
next game on December 1, the Red Wing freshman went one-
on-one with Calgary's Shean Donovan, who failed to convert
on his attempt with 1:11 remaining. Donovan never got his
shot off, but the Flames won 3–2.

2.14 C. A Canadian museum

One of the crown jewels in the auction of more than 50 Jacques
Plante hockey items, including trophies and Stanley Cup rings,
was Plante's 1960s pretzel-style mask, the third one used by
Plante in NHL play. The fibreglass, caramel-coloured mask,
first worn in 1963 after the netminder was traded to the New
York Rangers, was purchased by the Canadian Museum of
Civilization in Ottawa for almost U.S.$19,000. The Montreal
auction house Classic Collectables conducted the auction on
behalf of Plante's Swiss widow, Caroline Raymonde Plante. The
money raised went to a foundation to develop Swiss goalies.

2.15 C. Mike Dunham

Goalie Dunc Wilson's playoff stats were once considered an
anomaly among 250-game veterans. During his career, bad

timing—or just a knack for winding up on bad teams—netted Wilson zero minutes of playoff action and the goalie mark for most games without any postseason experience. But all that changed with netminders Mike Dunham, Roberto Luongo and Martin Biron, who challenged Wilson's 287-game mark with their own efforts in futility. During the 2006 postseason, Biron was still waiting for his first playoff start, after 281 career games. But Luongo and Dunham missed another postseason, backstopping 10th-place Atlanta and 11th-place Florida. Before stepping between the crease in 2006–07, Luongo worked 341 games, and Dunham, the all-time leader, 375 games, without a playoff match on their resumés.

2.16 A. Johnny Bower
According to the NHL's trivia registry, the last time the Toronto Maple Leafs recorded a shutout against New York was when Johnny Bower blanked the Rangers 6–0 on February 15, 1967. Almost 40 years and counting, it is the longest such streak in NHL history. No team has gone longer without blanking a rival.

2.17 C. 12 wins
Ray Emery was once only Dominik Hasek's backup. That lowly status changed in late 2005-06, when he became the team's future with his march through March campaign. Emery was named defensive player of the month and rookie of the month after leading all goaltenders with a 12–2–2 record, including two shutouts, a 2.09 goals-against average and .925 save-percentage. His 12 wins also tied a league record for most victories in a calendar month, set first by Philadelphia's Bernie Parent in March 1974.

Lockout Lingo

THE **DEFINITIVE** **QUOTE** of 2004–05's NHL labour dispute may be in the *2006 NHL Guide and Record Book*. Opposite the year 2004–05, atop the list of previous Stanley Cup winners and team rosters dating back to 1892, is the line "No Cup Winner." In this game, match the individuals below with their familiar quotes about hockey's longest lockout.

Solutions are on page 119

PART 1

Wayne Gretzky

Ottawa enforcer Rob Ray

L.A. Kings forward Sean Avery

Mike Lupica, the *New York Daily News*

Flyers goalie Robert Esche

TV host Jay Leno

Former NHL great Marcel Dionne

1. _____ "I think there are a lot of great owners out there, but there's a madman leading them down the wrong path."
2. _____ "Fans are disappointed, but the action is expected to save over 3,000 teeth."
3. _____ "I felt, OK, maybe Mario and I don't have the answers... I just feel disappointed and, quite frankly, I'm a little embarrassed."
4. _____ "I'd cross the line in a second. Why wouldn't I?"
5. _____ "Why should you pay a kid, coming out of junior, who hasn't done anything, a million bucks?"
6. _____ "I still say the (New York) Rangers haven't looked this good in the month of March since '94."

7. _____ "We burned a year for nothing. We didn't win anything. We didn't prove anything. We didn't get anything. We wasted an entire season."

PART 2

Flyers GM Bobby Clarke	Bob Goodenow
Greg Cote, the *Miami Herald*	Devils GM Lou Lamoriello
Gary Bettman	Jim Armstrong, the *Denver Post*

All-time minor-league goal leader Kevin Kerr

1. _____ "Players are not greedy."
2. _____ "Sure, a lot of people have been hurt by the NHL lockout, but the ones I really feel sorry for are Canadian. I mean, how much curling can a man take?"
3. _____ "I'll come and play for thirty grand and a jersey and meal money, just to say I had a chance to play in the NHL.... Maybe they'll realize what it means for some of us guys to play in the NHL."
4. _____ "Someone has to grab Goodenow by the throat and tell him, 'Look after the Canadian cities.' "
5. _____ "The NHL and its players are still meeting, with discussions now centring on a two-game regular season followed by a one-period sudden-death playoff."
6. _____ "All we have to do to solve [the problem] is to do what the cardinals are doing to get a new Pope. They are not leaving the room until there is white smoke."
7. _____ "If we don't have a new CBA, so that our players can start the season with us in October, we will not open on time."

3

Only the Firsts

MARIO LEMIEUX MAY BE famous for his first-game-first-shift first-shot goal in his 1984 debut, but Washington's Alexander Ovechkin is the only number one draft pick in league history to score a pair of goals in his NHL debut. Ovechkin refused to let his team lose, twice answering with goals, first on a slap shot and then on a wrist shot, and each time bulging the twine less than 90 seconds after his opponents took the lead. "I feel my dreams come true," Ovechkin said. "I play in the NHL. First game. First win." The 20-year-old Russian's dominance in Washington's 3–2 win against Columbus was a big sign of things to come.

Answers are on page 43

3.1 **Which player is usually credited with pioneering hockey's first slap shot?**

A. Alex Shibicky of the New York Rangers

B. Charlie Conacher of the Toronto Maple Leafs

C. Sweeney Schriner of the New York Americans

D. Bernie Geoffrion of the Montreal Canadiens

3.2 **In which NHL city did the first professional hockey game take place?**

A. Montreal

B. Toronto

C. Pittsburgh

D. Ottawa

3.3 **In 2003, who became the first hockey player to have a classical musical composition written about one of his goals?**

A. Bill Barilko

B. Bobby Orr

C. Wayne Gretzky

D. Peter Forsberg

3.4 **Who was the first player to speak out publicly against the NHL Players Association during the lockout of 2004–05?**

A. John Madden of the New Jersey Devils

B. Chris Chelios of the Detroit Red Wings

C. Mike Commodore of the Calgary Flames

D. Brett Hull of the Detroit Red Wings

3.5 **Who was the first high-profile player to walk away from the entire NHL season of 2004–05 because of the lockout?**

A. Markus Naslund

B. Peter Forsberg

C. Jaromir Jagr

D. Vincent Lecavalier

3.6 **Who is the only player to lead the NHL in penalty minutes in his first two seasons?**

A. Chris Nilan

B. Bob Probert

C. John Ferguson

D. Keith Magnuson

3.7 Who is the only NHL player to lead the league in power-play goals and shorthanded goals—in the same season—twice in his career?

A. Pavel Bure

B. Wayne Gretzky

C. Mario Lemieux

D. Jaromir Jagr

3.8 Who is the only player to score a goal in the NHL before he scored his first goal in junior hockey?

A. Kris Draper

B. Michel Goulet

C. Neal Broten

D. Jimmy Carson

3.9 Who is the first Canadian to coach in the Russian Super League?

A. Rick Bowness

B. Dave King

C. Michel Bergeron

D. Don Cherry

3.10 Who was the first NHLer to test positive for banned steroids?

A. Bryan Berard

B. Zdeno Chara

C. Matthew Barnaby

D. José Théodore

3.11 Complete the following quote by veteran NHL defenseman Mathieu Dandenault, who said after playing in his first game as a Montreal Canadien in 2005–06: "I don't really feel a part of Montreal yet," because "......................."

A. "I haven't moved into my condo."

B. "I haven't scored my first point here."

C. "I haven't won a Stanley Cup here."

D. "I haven't been booed yet."

3.12 Which Boston player was scratched from the lineup in January 1958, prompting the Bruins to call up minor leaguer Willie O'Ree—the first black man to play in the NHL?

A. Right-winger Leo Labine

B. Centre Bronco Horvath

C. Centre Don McKenney

D. Left-winger Johnny Bucyk

3.13 What professional hockey first did the Flyers' Antero Niittymaki accomplish while playing with the AHL Philadelphia Phantoms in April 2004?

A. He was the first European goalie with a 30-win season

B. He was the first pro goalie credited with an overtime goal

C. He was the first AHL goalie fined for illegal pads

D. He was the first pro goalie with a shootout win

3.14 Which enforcer publicly admitted, "I'm the first person to go through stage four in the substance abuse program and get back to hockey"?

A. Louie Debrusk

B. Dave Semenko

C. Bob Probert

D. Brantt Myhres

3.15 Who became the first NHL player to be awarded two penalty shots in one game in 2005-06?

    A. Erik Cole of the Carolina Hurricanes

    B. Milan Hejduk of the Colorado Avalanche

    C. Ryan Smyth of the Edmonton Oilers

    D. Mike Modano of the Dallas Stars

3.16 Which player scored the controversial shootout goal in 2005-06 that brought about a video review rule change?

    A. Brad Richards

    B. Jeremy Roenick

    C. Alexander Ovechkin

    D. Jussi Jokinen

3.17 Who is the first NHL rookie to lead the league in shots on goal since 1967-68?

    A. Guy Lafleur (in 1971-72)

    B. Mike Bossy (in 1977-78)

    C. Wayne Gretzky (in 1979-80)

    D. Alexander Ovechkin (in 2005-06)

3.18 In what year did a Zamboni first appear on NHL ice?

    A. 1949

    B. 1955

    C. 1961

    D. 1967

Answers

3.1 **A. Alex Shibicky of the New York Rangers**

The first slap shot has many claimants. Although Bernie Geoffrion is often credited with being the first player to use it, almost two decades before the Boomer unleashed his shot, Alex Shibicky was winding up and blasting his own slappers. "It was a snap shot from the hip," according to his son, Alex Jr. Shibicky caught on with the Rangers in 1935–36 and was almost immediately teamed with linemates Neil and Mac Colville. The trio learned every detail of the game from veterans Bill and Bun Cook, including an innovative technique for shooting the puck that Shibicky first tried in practice, then pioneered in a game in 1937. But Shibicky's claim is also not without its challengers, including Bun Cook, who may also have used the slap shot in game play. Shibicky, however, is adamant that "Bun never used the slapper in a game. I did, but it was his idea." Still, no matter who was first, Shibicky's unit soon clicked, and it was dubbed the Bread Line by sportswriters who called the trio the "bread and butter" of the Rangers. And in 1940, with the Bread Line and the Cook brothers firing on all cylinders, New York won the Stanley Cup, its last championship before Mark Messier led the Blueshirts to 1994's Cup. When Shibicky died in July 2005, the NHL made plans to send the Stanley Cup to the Vancouver area to commemorate his accomplishments.

3.2   C. Pittsburgh

It may be one of hockey's most unbelievable believe-it-or-not facts. More than a decade before the NHL was founded in 1917–18, and years before any other pro league started up, a small and short-lived league called the International Hockey League operated a five-team circuit that paid salaries to its players. In its inaugural game on December 9, 1904, a Portage Lakes team from Houghton, Michigan, beat hometown Pittsburgh 6–3. The first pro goal ever was scored by Barney Holden of Portage Lakes. At the time, the Stanley Cup was awarded to the best amateur team and players, most of whom wanted to earn money playing the game they loved. Some played for one of the five original IHL teams: Pittsburgh; Sault Ste. Marie, Ontario; and Michigan's Sault Ste. Marie, Portage Lakes and Calumet. The league's top recruits included Hall of Famers Fred "Cyclone" Taylor and Joe Hall.

3.3   B. Bobby Orr

"The Goal," a musical tribute to Orr's famous 1970 Stanley Cup-winning goal, was performed for the first time on July 18, 2003, at the 2003 Festival of the Sound—Parry Sound, Ontario's annual classical music festival. Orr, who was born in Parry Sound, was in the audience to hear the piece, which was composed by Eric Robertson for brass quintet and narrator. The tribute was part of the grand opening of the new Charles W. Stockey Centre for the Performing Arts and the Bobby Orr Hall of Fame.

3.4   A. John Madden of the New Jersey Devils

Even though the NHLPA was quick to admonish players who openly admitted to considering a salary cap, a fair number still stepped forward, the first being John Madden on the first day of the lockout. "The only problem I'm having with things is believing whose numbers are right and whose numbers are wrong. Those are the big issues. And if it needs to have a cap, give it a cap, you know?" Madden told the Newark *Star-Ledger*. The next day, Madden skated around the issue, reworking his comments to say that he would support his union in the event that it accepted a cap.

3.5   B. Peter Forsberg

Less than a week after NHL commissioner Gary Bettman indefinitely postponed the 2004–05 season, starting September 15, 2004, 155 NHLers began playing in Europe. The most notable among that group? Peter Forsberg, who signed on September 18 to play with his old club, MoDo, in the Swedish Elite League. The Colorado Avalanche centre committed to the entire season, irregardless of any settlement in the labour dispute. "It has always been my dream to come back and play for my home team and win a championship," said Forsberg, who certainly wasn't there to match his NHL income, considering his reported $22,000-a-month salary. Forsberg received a hero's welcome in Sweden, but he played just 33 games and earned a 13–26–39 record before breaking his wrist on January 20, 2005. MoDo failed to win its championship, a feat the club last performed in 1979.

3.6   D. Keith Magnuson

Keith Magnuson didn't win many fights during his career, but he would fearlessly throw punches with anyone. After breaking into the NHL with Chicago in 1969–70, the hard-nosed defenseman racked up 100 or more penalty minutes in each of his first six seasons and led the loop in his rookie and sophomore seasons with 213 and 291 PIM, respectively, a feat no other NHLer has duplicated. A fan favourite and team leader, Magnuson adopted coach Billy Reay's defensive mantra of "None Against," striving at all costs to keep the puck out of his own net. Selected in 2001 as a member of the Blackhawks' 75th-anniversary All-Star team, Magnuson died in a car accident on December 15, 2003.

3.7 C. Mario Lemieux

There are power-play specialists and there are penalty-killing specialists, and then there are a few rare individuals, such as Mario Lemieux, who excel as both. The Magnificent One led the NHL with 31 power-play and 13 shorthanded goals in 1988–89. In 1995–96, the Penguins superstar duplicated the feat, topping the league with 31 power-play goals and eight shorthanded tallies.

3.8 A. Kris Draper

A combination of unusual circumstances allowed Kris Draper to score a goal in the NHL before he had played a single game in junior hockey. Draper joined the Canadian National hockey team on a full-time basis at age 17 in 1988–89. The following season he was selected 62nd overall in the 1989 NHL Entry Draft by the Winnipeg Jets and, on October 4, 1990, made his NHL debut with a goal against the Toronto Maple Leafs. After playing two more NHL games, Draper was sent down to the Ottawa 67s of the Ontario Hockey League, where he scored 19 goals in 39 games. As well, later that season Draper played seven games for Moncton in the AHL, where he scored twice.

3.9 B. Dave King

It's not easy living in a steel town on the banks of the Ural River, even for Russians used to such hardships. So what would possess Dave King, former NHL bench boss and three-time coach of Canada's Olympic team, to move there to coach the Metallurg Magnitogorsk? Ever a student of the game, King saw the chance to study Russian elite hockey from the inside. And his tutorial was relatively painless. He had the chance to coach the best young hockey player outside the NHL, Evgeni Malkin. And, after learning a smattering of "cue" words and phrases so he could coach in Russian, by mid-season of 2005–06, King had Metallurg in first place. His experiences won't be forgotten, either—a book is forthcoming.

3.10 A. Bryan Berard

This is not the kind of first any athlete wants on his record. But Bryan Berard will forever be remembered as the first NHLer busted for steroid use, after testing positive for the banned substance 19-norandrosterone in November 2005. Ironically, Berard did not face disciplinary measures from the NHL because the test was not part of the league's program. Rather, as a U.S. Olympic team candidate, Berard was caught by the U.S. Anti-Doping Agency and barred from international hockey for two years. Of the 250 athletes tested who were eligible for Olympic teams, Berard was the only one to test positive. (Later, during pre-Olympic drug testing in January 2006, José Théodore tested positive for a hair restoration drug known as Propecia, a prescription product that is banned as a masking agent.) "No question, I'm embarrassed about it," said Berard, who claims the steroid was contained in a supplement he took to get ready for the 2005–06 NHL season.

3.11 D. "I haven't been booed yet."

He said it with a grin, but Mathieu Dandedault knows how harsh the media spotlight can be on a French player with the

Canadiens, and how fast Montreal's loyal fans can jump on an underachiever. That kind of attention turned his defensive predecessor, the much-maligned Patrice Brisebois, into a human bull's-eye, finally forcing him into hockey anonymity in blissful Denver. As one Montreal headline stated: If you haven't been booed, you're not a Canadien. Patrick Roy was driven out of town by boos one fateful night in 1995, and Hall of Famer Bernie Geoffrion still remembers the boos he received for having the gall to win the scoring title from Maurice Richard in 1955. Tough crowd, those Frenchies.

3.12   A. Right-winger Leo Labine

Willie O'Ree is often called the Jackie Robinson of hockey for being the first black player in the NHL. But for all his on-ice talent, he never impacted the sport like Robinson, who broke the colour barrier and cleared a path for thousands of black ballplayers to follow. O'Ree was simply the first. Yes, it was a courageous act, but, despite O'Ree's efforts to prove that he belonged in the NHL, no other black athlete played in the league until 1974, when Mike Marson was drafted by Washington. O'Ree's big break came on January 18, 1958, when the Bruins' hard-hitting winger Leo Labine was laid low by the flu and O'Ree played left wing on a line with Don McKenney and Jerry Toppazzini. Within two games, O'Ree was back with the Quebec Aces, arguably hockey's best team outside the NHL. O'Ree's historic rise to hockey supremacy is compelling because he played with only one eye—and hid the injury well enough to sustain a 21-year pro career. Even so, O'Ree faced no challenge greater than the prejudice against the colour of his skin. In February 1998, he was named director of youth development for NHL Diversity.

3.13   **B. He was the first pro goalie credited with an overtime goal**

They've scored game-winners and power-play goals and recorded shutouts while scoring a goal, but until Antero Niittymaki, no netminder had ever potted an overtime goal—or a shorthanded one. Niittymaki managed both at once on April 11, 2004, in a game between the Hershey Bears and Philadelphia Phantoms of the AHL. With the teams deadlocked 2–2 midway through overtime, Hershey coach Paul Fixter pulled goaltender Phillippe Sauve during a power play in a last-game gamble to qualify for the Calder Cup playoffs. But the five-on-three-man advantage failed during the ensuing attack when Shane Willis's wild pass back to the point left the Phantom zone, rebounded off the boards at centre ice and slid into Hershey's vacated net. Niittymaki was the last Philadelphia player to play the puck and was credited with the OT goal.

3.14   **D. Brantt Myhres**

Hockey tough guy Brantt Myhres's worst foe has always been his own demons. After a 154-game, 687-penalty-minute career in the NHL, he hit the league's limit of four go-arounds in its substance abuse program: 28 days the first time; then two months, six months and, finally, a full year of rehab that forced Myhres to miss all of 2003–04. It's safe to say Myhres was a very good active alcoholic, conning the system until stage four—his last shot at playing and staying sober. The bottle has long been considered an occupational hazard with heavyweights (because of the stress in fighting for a living), but don't expect Myhres—the recovering alcoholic—to be a pacifist on-ice. In an AHL game on December 11, 2004, he received an eight-game suspension after an ugly bench-clearing brawl between Lowell and Norfolk. As of 2005–06, Myhres was playing for the AHL's Omaha Ak-Sar-Ben Knights.

3.15 A. Erik Cole of the Carolina Hurricanes

Eric Cole became the first player with two penalty shots in one NHL game, scoring on the first as the Hurricanes chalked up a franchise-record eighth straight victory, a 5–3 win over the Buffalo Sabres on November 9, 2005. The Carolina winger was awarded the first shot while his club was shorthanded in the third period, after being hauled down from behind by Jochen Hecht. The goal gave the Hurricanes a 4–1 lead. Later in the third, Cole was hooked by Dmitri Kalinin and granted another penalty shot, which was foiled by goalie Martin Biron. "I made the move I wanted, but not the shot I wanted," said Cole. In his next game, two nights later, Cole earned yet another penalty shot. But he couldn't beat Florida's Roberto Luongo.

3.16 B. Jeremy Roenick

Hockey would be something less than it is without Jeremy Roenick. The skating mouthpiece with the flashy hockey skills brings opinion, drama and passion to the game every night. Not surprisingly, he is also no stranger to controversy. So Roenick's move to Los Angeles in 2005–06 seemed inspired, except for the fact it produced one of his lowest scoring seasons. Among the highlights was his controversial shootout goal against Nashville on November 5, 2005. Replays showed Roenick scored on a rebound by playing the puck twice in a fall that sent Predator goalie Tomas Vokoun into the net with the puck. The NHL later made the first in-season rule change to allow video reviews of shootouts.

3.17 D. Alexander Ovechkin (in 2005–06)

Only the combination of a once-in-a-generation player on a scoring-challenged team in rebuilding mode, playing under nearly obstruction-free rules, could produce such an NHL first. Along with numerous other NHL and franchise rookie records, Washington's Alexander Ovechkin broke the league rookie mark for most shots in a season. In a 4–3 loss to Carolina on April 5, 2006, he recorded five shots to give him 388, one more than Teemu Selanne's mark of 387 in 1992–93. Then, with seven games remaining in the Capitals' schedule, Ovechkin notched another 37 for a league-best 425 shots in 2005–06. Ovechkin is the only rookie to top all players in one season since shot counts were first tabulated in 1967–68, his highest total coming against Tampa Bay on March 23, 2006, when he tallied 13 shots. It's not an official record, but is considered the most by any player since Brian Leetch's 13 in a game against Washington, January 4, 1989. (Ray Bourque is said to have netted an unofficial record of 19 against Quebec on March 21, 1991.)

3.18 B. 1955
The Zamboni was invented in 1945 by Frank Zamboni, a rink attendant at Paramount Studios in Hollywood, California. His idea of a motorized ice-cleaner caught the attention of figure skater Sonja Jenje, and with her support, Zamboni was able to build a prototype. (Before the Zamboni, NHL rinks were cleaned and flooded between periods by workers using shovels and barrels of water.) The Zamboni made its NHL debut on March 10, 1955, in a 0–0 tie between the Canadiens and the Maple Leafs at the Montreal Forum. It was a bumpy baptism. During the game, Habs fans grew so angry with the Leafs' stifling, defensive play that they littered the ice with garbage, including pigs feet.

3

The Triggermen

IT'S NOT ALWAYS THE top goal scorers or point earners who lead the NHL in shots on goal each season. Sometimes the league's leading triggermen aren't even in the top 10; and, in rare cases, the winner might be a defenseman. Listed below are several shots-on-goal champions, dating back to 1967–68, when the statistic was first tabulated. Match the champs in the left column with their shot number and season on the right. It's not as hard as it looks if you use the year to your advantage.

Solutions are on page 120

PART 1

1._____	Ilya Kovalchuk	A. 340 shots in 1983–84
2._____	Darryl Sittler	B. 311 shots in 1977–78
3._____	Ray Bourque	C. 341 shots in 2003–04
4._____	Brett Hull	D. 429 shots in 1998–99
5._____	Pavel Bure	E. 384 shots in 2000–01
6._____	Paul Kariya	F. 384 shots in 1974–75
7._____	Bobby Orr	G. 408 shots in 1991–92

PART 2

1._____	Phil Esposito	A. 348 shots in 1979–80
2._____	Bill Guerin	B. 369 shots in 1981–82
3._____	Brendan Shanahan	C. 397 shots in 1993–94
4._____	Marcel Dionne	D. 364 shots in 1967–68
5._____	Jaromir Jagr	E. 550 shots in 1970–71
6._____	Bobby Hull	F. 355 shots in 2001–02
7._____	Wayne Gretzky	G. 403 shots in 1995–96

4

True or False?

UNTIL TIE DOMI WAS honoured at the Air Canada Centre for his 1,000th game on March 4, 2006, his mother, Meryem, had never seen him play at the NHL level. True or False? *True.* It was an emotional night for Tie Domi, one of the few tough guys to ever hit the NHL's 1,000-game plateau. As a tribute to his late father, Domi requested that the national anthem be sung by Tom Cochrane. Then, in a pre-game ceremony that had the fans on their feet, Domi was joined by his wife, two children and mother, Meryem, who had never before seen him play an NHL game. "I don't call you guys fans, I call you friends," Domi told the crowd. Unfortunately, Domi's big night was spoiled as Toronto lost to Ottawa 4–2. Domi played 13:05 without a point or penalty. His 1,000th game was played the previous night in Buffalo.

Answers are on page 57

4.1 **Prior to Alexander Ovechkin, no player had ever been named NHL player of the month and rookie of the month in the same month.** True or False?

4.2 **The Calder Trophy for rookie of the year is the only NHL trophy a player can win once in his career.** True or False?

4.3 As of 2006, Paul Henderson, the scoring hero of the 1972 Summit Series between Canada and Russia, has not been inducted into the Hockey Hall of Fame. True or False?

4.4 Gordie Howe is the oldest player to appear in a game for the Detroit Red Wings. True or False?

4.5 Neither of the two players whose sweater numbers are retired by the Phoenix Coyotes ever played for that club. True or False?

4.6 Former NHL goon Stu Grimson graduated from law school after retiring in 2001–02. True or False?

4.7 Daniel and Henrik Sedin, selected second and third overall by the Vancouver Canucks at the 1999 entry draft, are the highest drafted brothers in NHL history. True or False?

4.8 NHL players can only play with hockey sticks made by manufacturers that have paid a licensing fee to the National Hockey League. True or False?

4.9 In June 2004, the *Tampa Tribune* ran an editorial stating that the Lightning had lost Game 7 of the Stanley Cup finals. True or False?

4.10 No team in NHL history has ever come to New York and beat all three New York-metropolitan-area clubs—the Rangers, Islanders and Devils—in succession. True or False?

4.11 No rookie has ever scored his first NHL goal in overtime. True or False?

4.12 Anson Carter wore sweater No. 77 with Vancouver in 2005–06 to pay homage to one-time teammates Ray Bourque and Adam Oates. True or False?

4.13 When comparing the average ages of NHLers from year to year, players in 2005–06 were older than at any time in recent memory. True or False?

4.14 Every time the New York Rangers have held a ceremony to retire a player's jersey number, they have won the game. True or False?

4.15 Among the items sold at Bobby Hull's 2004 auction were his false teeth. True or False?

4.16 Among active goalies in 2005–06, Martin Brodeur had been with the NHL franchise that drafted him longer than any other netminder. True or False?

4.17 Darryl Sutter and his son Brett were both drafted 179th overall in their respective years. True or False?

4.18 Counting playoffs, Dave Andreychuk played in more NHL games before winning his first Stanley Cup than Ray Bourque. True or False?

4.19 In 33 years of officiating a record 2,906 NHL games, linesman Ray Scapinello never missed a game because of injury. True or False?

4.20 Based on BBM television ratings, the 2004 World Cup of Hockey finals between Canada and Finland finished *second* to *Survivor: Vanuatu* in hockey-mad Vancouver. True or False?

4.21 No player on Calgary's 1989 Stanley Cup-winning team was with the original team during its first year in the city, 1980–81. True or False?

4.22 Hockey visors do not affect a player's vision. True or False?

4.23 Toronto's Mats Sundin collected his 1,100th NHL point before he played in his 1,100th career game. True or False?

4.24 Although Boston, Toronto, Chicago, Detroit, New York and Montreal are known as "Original Six" teams, they are not the original founding clubs of the NHL. True or False?

4.25 Engraved on the Stanley Cup are names of teams that never won the Cup. True or False?

4.26 The silhouetted player in the new International Ice Hockey Federation logo is NHL star Mats Sundin. True or False?

4.27 No member of the 2005–06 Phoenix Coyotes was with the Winnipeg Jets in 1995–96, the last season before the Canadian team relocated to Arizona. True or False?

4.28 Chris Chelios's fourth Winter Olympics in 2006 is a record by an NHLer. True or False?

Answers

4.1 **False**

Since the inception of the Rookie of the Month Award in 1983–84, only three NHLers have won the double distinction of top player and rookie honours in the same month. Alexander Ovechkin, who notched both awards in January 2006 after scoring a league-leading 21 points in 14 games (11–10–21), joined Washington Capitals goalie Jim Carey (March 1995) and Winnipeg Jets winger Teemu Selanne (January 1993). Ovechkin, who had seven multiple-point games, recorded his first hat trick on January 13 in a 3–2 overtime win against Anaheim, and scored what became known as the Goal while rolling on his back at full speed against Phoenix in a 6–1 win on January 16. His numbers speak even more to the anaemic play of the Capitals. He netted 28 per cent of the Capitals' goals and earned points on 53 per cent of the team's goals, 21 of 40. Washington won five and lost 10 games that month.

4.2 **True**

By definition, the Calder is a one-time trophy for a player, awarded to the NHL's top rookie. The winner is chosen by the Professional Hockey Writers' Association, but the honour confers no guarantee of a stellar career. Still, despite such Calder-winner flops as Willi Plett, Steve Vickers and Brit Selby, the association's track record at predicting future stars has been surprisingly accurate, including such notable Calder winners as Dany Heatley, Peter Forsberg and Martin Brodeur.

4.3 **True**

Paul Henderson may have scored the biggest goal in
Canadian hockey history, but that hasn't swayed Hall voters
to induct the 13-year NHL veteran. Henderson's winning goal
on September 28, 1972, with 34 seconds left in Game 8 of the
Summit Series, gave Canada a 6–5 win in the series' deciding
game. But it's not as if Henderson's heroics in Moscow have
been forgotten. Henderson is a member of the Canadian
Sports Hall of Fame and his famous goal has been honoured
by a Canada Post commemorative stamp and a silver coin
issued by the Royal Canadian Mint. Meanwhile, two members of the 1972 Soviet squad are Hall of Famers. Vladislav
Tretiak was inducted in 1989 and Valeri Kharlamov in 2005.

4.4 **False**

When Chris Chelios played in 2005–06's season opener in
Detroit against the St. Louis Blues on October 5, he was 43
years, 253 days old. Gordie Howe was 43 years and four days
old in his last Red Wing game in 1971. When asked if he
thinks about his age, Chelios said, "Only every time I think
about Gordie Howe."

4.5 **True**

You can move the franchise but you can't change its history. Phoenix's past is undeniably linked not only to its NHL
days when the team played in Winnipeg as the Jets, but to
its inception as a WHA club named after the signing of the
Golden Jet, Bobby Hull, in 1972. Ten years after the moving
trucks rolled out of Winnipeg in 1996, Coyote records are still
dotted with Jet players and Glendale Arena sports banners
honouring Hull's No. 9 and Thomas Steen's No. 25. Neither
number has ever appeared on a Coyote jersey, but in 2005–06,

the old numbers were again in the public eye. Brett Hull was handed his father's famous No. 9 when he signed with the club, and No. 25 was officially placed in the club's ring of honour at a ceremony on January 21, 2006. Bobby Hull played seven seasons with the Jets in the WHA, but only 18 games after the team joined the NHL. Steen's entire 950-game career was spent in Winnipeg.

4.6 True

Tough guys aren't all mindless ice goons. Stu Grimson, the Grim Reaper of blood, mayhem and 2,113 penalty minutes during his 12-year NHL career, surprised players and fans when he announced his graduation from law school in 2005. Fellow students at the University of Memphis were equally taken aback—but because of Grimson's previous occupation as an NHL thug. "Some of my students say: 'Golly, we've seen video of him beating the heck out of someone.' That's difficult to believe," said Donna Harkness, University of Memphis professor of clinical law. "That was a shock. He just does not have that kind of aura now at all." Grimson's Jekyll and Hyde act is a permanent transformation. He joined the NHL players union in 2006.

4.7 False

At second and third overall, the Sedin twins were high draft picks, but not the highest brother combo of all time. In 1983, the Hartford Whalers took Sylvain Turgeon second overall. In 1987, the Buffalo Sabres picked his younger brother, Pierre, first overall. The Sedins will have a tough time matching the Turgeon brothers' scoring prowess. Sylvain netted 269 career goals; Pierre surpassed the 500-goal plateau in 2005–06.

4.8 False

Although NHLers can choose from a half-dozen major stick-makers licensed by the league, they can also play with a non-licensed stick, though only if the logo is blacked out on the shaft.

4.9 True

"Stop the presses" should have been the rallying cry after the Tampa Bay Lightning won the Stanley Cup in 2004. The *Tribune* had prepared two editorials—one for a win and one for a loss. But despite the correct text being placed in the paper's computers, the editorial that appeared in 275,000 copies of the *Tribune* opened with: "The Tampa Bay Lightning didn't win the National Hockey League's Stanley Cup last night. But the team had a championship season nevertheless." The correct editorial, which never made ink, credited the Lightning for generating pride and excitement in the community.

4.10 False

It's a rare hat trick by NHL standards. As of 2003–04, only 16 franchises on 39 occasions have played consecutive games against all three New York-area teams, and among those visitors, only the Los Angeles Kings in 2001–02 went home with three wins. The Kings beat the Islanders 3–0, the Devils 3–2 and the Rangers 4–0 between January 5 and 9. However, the three teams of the Big Apple and suburbs have cooperated on four occasions to blank visiting clubs, including the Vancouver Canucks, who have made a record nine swings through the New York area. In 2005–06, the Florida Panthers lost three in a row while on tour, with defeats to the Devils (3–0), the Islanders (4–3) and the Rangers (4–0), January 3 to 7.

4.11 **False**

It may not be a league first, but Brent Seabrook still made quite an impression on his first NHL goal. The rookie defenseman earned a 6–5 win for Chicago after the Blackhawks had blown a three-goal lead in the third period on November 2, 2005. Seabrook fired a wrist shot past the Blues' Patrick Lalime just 35 seconds into overtime. "It's awesome," Seabrook said. "I'm thrilled right now. I'm going to keep that puck."

4.12 **False**

Anson Carter has a long and uninterrupted history with duplicate digits. In Boston he donned Nos. 11 and 33, No. 22 with Edmonton, New York and Washington and No. 11 in Los Angeles. But when he signed with the Canucks in August 2005, No. 22 was on Daniel Sedin's back, No. 33 belonged to Henrik Sedin, Todd Bertuzzi had dibs on No. 44 and Ed Jovanovski owned No. 55. Since Mario Lemieux's retired No. 66 wasn't an option, Carter finally settled on No. 77.

4.13 **True**

Conditioning, nutrition, rehabilitation and a generally larger population have increased the average size and age of NHL players. During Bobby Hull's era, players averaged five-foot-11 (211 cm), 184.5 pounds (83 kg) and 26.4 years. More than 30 years later, in 2005–06, NHLers have grown two inches (5 cm), bulked up by 20 pounds (nine kg) and added two years to their careers. If Hull is yesterday's player, Marian Hossa, at six-foot-one (185 cm), 208 pounds (94 kg) and 27 years, is today's version of average. Based on first-game rosters of the NHL's 30 clubs, Hossa represents today's typical six-foot-one (185-cm), 205-pound (92-kg) player with an average age of 28.4 years, older than at any time since 1972–73.

4.14 **False**

The Rangers may get the crowds for the ceremony, but they can't seem to get the goals for a win when they retire a player's number. New York is only 1–3 when they raise a sweater at Madison Square Garden. The Blueshirts lost to Washington 5–3 on October 14, 1979, following the retirement of Rod Gilbert's No. 7; lost 6–3 to Winnipeg when Ed Giacomin's No. 1 was hoisted on March 15, 1989; were defeated 4–3 by the Minnesota Wild on February 4, 2004, when Mike Richter's No. 35 went up; and earned a 5–4 victory against Edmonton to celebrate No. 11 on Mark Messier night, January 12, 2006, which came on a shootout goal by Jaromir Jagr. Even in retirement Messier could inspire.

4.15 **True**

One of the more bizarre items on the block at Bobby Hull's collectibles auction in 2004 was his partial upper plate. The famous choppers of Hull's trademark smile were apparently lost during a trip to Switzerland in the 1950s and later mailed back to him. When the booty from the auction was finally counted, the Golden Jet's false teeth had fetched U.S.$575.96.

4.16 **False**

In 2005–06, only Steve Yzerman and Mike Modano had been with their drafted clubs longer than netminder Olaf Kolzig, who was selected by Washington 19th overall in 1989. Many expected Kolzig to be traded during the Capitals' salary dump of 2004, but a deal never materialized, keeping him ahead of Martin Brodeur (Brodeur was selected by New Jersey 20th overall in 1990, the year after Kolzig's draft year).

4.17   **True**

Louis Sutter sired an unprecedented six NHL-playing sons,
who between them played a total of almost 5,000 games—
5,603 games, if you include the playoffs. Neither the Howes,
Hulls, Richards, Hunters nor Stastnys can claim the legacy
of the Sutters in NHL action, including their 1,320 goal count,
2,935 point total and 7,224 minutes in box time. During a
five-year span in the 1980s, all six brothers were playing in
the league at the same time. Louis Sutter, who passed away
in February 2005, saw all of his six sons working in the NHL
after retiring as players. And now, his grandsons are showing
potential, including Darryl's son Brett, who was drafted by
Calgary 179th overall—the same draft position his father held
27 years earlier in Chicago, in 1978.

4.18   **False**

Both Ray Bourque and Dave Andreychuk became sentimen-
tal choices to win the Stanley Cup during the final seasons
of their long and storied careers. Each won the Cup in their
22nd season: Bourque after 1,826 games and Andreychuk
after 1,759 games.

4.19   **True**

When Ray Scapinello was set to retire after the Stanley Cup
playoffs in 2004, his amazing longevity became public knowl-
edge. Scapinello, *the* NHL ironman, never missed a match
because of injury or sickness during his 2,906-game career
and, since 1971, logged more ice time than Gordie Howe and
handled more pucks than Wayne Gretzky. The five-foot-seven
(170-cm), 165-pound (74-kg) Scapinello credits his durability to
"dumb luck," which might have some validity considering he
didn't wear a helmet and broke up fights between opponents

who were less than half his age, 40 pounds (18 kg) heavier and almost a foot (30 cm) taller. According to Scapinello, the biggest changes in the last three decades have been the million-dollar salaries and the speed and fitness of players.

4.20   True

In Vancouver, the number one TV show during the week of September 13–19, 2004, was *Survivor: Vanuatu,* with an AMA (average minute audience) of 495,000—compared to the World Cup finals' 453,000. The hockey numbers were likely down because the game started at 4 PM in B.C., when most people were still at work. In Toronto, like the rest of Canada (except Quebec), viewers were much more interested in watching Mario Lemieux celebrate than which preening beach brat won *Survivor's* immunity idol. Quebeckers love their homegrown shows as much as NHL hockey, but not nearly as much when the international game is on the box. The World Cup finished number 17 for the week in la belle province.

4.21   False

One player from the first Calgary Flames team in 1980–81 was still with the club when it won the Cup eight seasons later in 1989: co-captain Jim Peplinski. Ironically, in the deciding sixth game of the Cup finals, coach Terry Crisp scratched the popular captain from the lineup, denying Peplinski the opportunity of being in uniform for the Cup presentation.

4.22   True

In 2004, researchers at Université de Montreal's School of Optometry subjected visors to a battery of eye tests with state-of-the-art equipment to determine any significant difference between the ability to see with or without a visor. The researchers recruited 18 amateur hockey players—10 men and eight women—to complete a series of tests three times: once wearing an Itech visor, once wearing an Oakley visor and once without a visor. The conclusions were clear: Visors in no way affect visual perception, colour contrast or peripheral vision. But don't expect the results to change many minds. It was Eric Lindros who compared wearing a visor to "driving in a rainstorm without windshield wipers."

4.23 True

Throughout his NHL career, Mats Sundin's point production has kept almost perfect pace with his career game count. He is the ultimate point-a-game player. Two games after collecting his 1,100th point, an assist against Montreal on November 26, Sundin played in his 1,100th career game on November 30 in Tampa Bay. As a Maple Leaf, Sundin played in his 800th game on January 28, 2006, and earned his 800th Maple Leaf point, a goal, five weeks later on March 7.

4.24 True

There was nothing "original" about the Original Six except for the Toronto Maple Leafs and Montreal Canadiens, two of the five founding members of the NHL in 1917–18. After that first season, the league soon ballooned into a 10-team circuit with franchises in markets such as Pittsburgh, St. Louis and Ottawa. Both Montreal and New York had two NHL teams, each competing in the same market. When the Brooklyn Americans folded in 1941, the league downsized to six teams and went on a 25-year hiatus from expansion, the era fondly remembered as the golden age of hockey with the Original Six teams. It lasted from 1941–42 to 1966–67.

4.25 **True**

Early Stanley Cup winners sometimes had their Cup opponent's name engraved alongside their own. In 1915, when
the Montreal Canadiens of the NHA beat the west coast rival
Portland Rosebuds (champions of the PCHA, 3–2 in the finals),
both teams were acknowledged for their play in the Cup. The
team engraving on the shoulder of the original Cup reads:
Canadian N.H.A. & World Champions, defeated Portland 1915–16.

4.26 **True**

After the IIHF introduced its new logo in 2005, inquiries about
the image of the silhouetted player (skating on top of a globe)
revealed that the model for the design was Mats Sundin. "We
took the picture right out of the Leafs' media guide," con-
fessed IIHF media director Szymon Szemberg. Alert hockey
fans will notice that while Sundin is a right shot, the logo's
silhouetted player is shooting left. Szemberg said the image
was reversed to work with the logo design.

4.27 **False**

When the wrecker's ball demolished the ancient Winnipeg
Arena in March 2006, the only Coyote still tied to Phoenix's
former club was 29-year-old centre Shane Doan, who joined
the Jets in their final NHL season, 1995–96, after being drafted
seventh overall by the club in 1995. "Those are huge moments
that I'll always remember," Doan recalled of his rookie
campaign in the old barn. Doan has been with Winnipeg–
Phoenix ever since.

4.28 **False**

Chris Chelios and Keith Tkachuk were the first four-time
Olympians in U.S. hockey history when they played at the

Torino Games in 2006. But for Chelios to set the all-time record, his Gordie Howe-like stamina needs to last until the 2014 Olympics—quite unlikely, considering Chelios will be 52 years old by then. Tkachuk, 10 years younger, has a chance at the record, but will he have the legs? For inspiration, the pair can turn to Raimo Helminen, who represented Finland in hockey at a record six Olympics between Sarajevo in 1984 and Salt Lake City in 2002. While Chelios and Helminen both began their Olympic careers in 1984, Chelios missed three Winter Games—in 1988 in Calgary, 1992 in Albertville and 1994 in Lillehammer—playing NHL hockey. Helminen played in every Olympic tournament, competing in his last when he was 37 years old. Had the NHL instituted Olympic breaks during Chelios's prime, the Detroit defenseman would have participated in his seventh Olympics at Torino. Now, *that's* inspiring.

The Best Rookie Class Ever?

FOR THE FIRST TIME in league history, rookies from two NHL Entry Drafts became available at the same time in one regular season. Blame the 2004–05 lockout for the embarrassment of riches in freshman talent and the plethora of records and firsts these newbies established in 2005–06. With such depth, it may be the best rookie class ever. But it comes with an asterisk, considering the lockout doubled the influx of first-year players. Match the 11 rookies with their records below. Pay attention, some set more than one mark.

Solutions are on page 120

Sidney Crosby	Marek Svatos	Alexander Ovechkin
Dion Phaneuf	Jussi Jokinen	Josh Harding
Henrik Lundqvist	Ray Emery	Kari Lehtonen
Ryan Miller		Antero Niittymaki

1. _____ He set an NHL rookie record for most shots on goal in one season.

2. _____ He is the first goalie to play his first NHL game and record his first win in a shootout.

3. _____ He is the youngest player in NHL history to score 90 *and* 100 points.

4. _____ He is only the third rookie defenseman to reach the 20-goal plateau in one season.

5. _____ He is the second rookie in NHL history to record 50 goals and 100 points in one season.

6. _____ He set the New York Rangers record for most wins by a rookie goalie.

7. _____ He is the first rookie to lead an NHL regular season in shots on goal.

8. _____ He tied the NHL rookie record with nine game-winning goals in one season.

9. _____ He is second in most points by a rookie who entered the league in the same year he was drafted.

10._____ He led all players in shootout goals during 2005–06.

11. _____ He recorded the best save-percentage in shootouts during 2005–06.

12._____ He is only the fourth rookie in NHL history to reach the 50-goal mark in one season.

13._____ He tied the league record for most goaltending victories in a calendar month.

14._____ They are the first two rookies in NHL history to score 100 points in a single season.

15._____ These five rookie goalies equalled the league record for most freshmen, with 20 wins in one season.

5

Taking *H*ome Gold

WE ALL KNOW WHAT happened. It's just that no one predicted it. Canada, the Olympic favourite, had depth at every position. Team USA was old but experienced. The Europeans turned the world on its ear with their well-prepared teams of skilled attackers and defenders. The 2006 Olympics in Torino, Italy, held many surprises and produced several revelations in its showcase of the world's best-on-best competition.

Answers are on page 75

5.1 **Which team won the gold medal in men's hockey at the 2006 Olympics?**
   A. Sweden
   B. Canada
   C. Finland
   D. USA

5.2 **What was the largest number of players from one NHL team on an Olympic squad in 2006?**
   A. Six players
   B. Eight players

C. 10 players

D. 12 players

5.3 Which NHL team iced the most Team Canada members at the Olympics?

A. The Tampa Bay Lightning

B. The Ottawa Senators

C. The Calgary Flames

D. The Colorado Avalanche

5.4 Among the 23 players on Team USA's roster, how many were making their Olympic debut?

A. Four players

B. Seven players

C. 10 players

D. 13 players

5.5 Which team ended Canada's hopes of repeating as Olympic gold medalists in 2006?

A. Switzerland

B. Russia

C. Finland

D. Sweden

5.6 Which country produced the two top scorers in men's hockey at the 2006 Winter Games?

A. Sweden

B. Russia

C. Finland

D. Slovakia

5.7 How many goals did Canada's women score and allow in their Olympic gold-medal showing in 2006?

A. 26 goals scored; 22 goals allowed

B. 33 goals scored; 15 goals allowed

C. 39 goals scored; nine goals allowed

D. 46 goals scored; two goals allowed

5.8 Which men's team had the oldest average age at the 2006 Olympics?

A. Team USA

B. Team Czech Republic

C. Team Canada

D. Team Sweden

5.9 At what age did the oldest player participate in Olympic hockey?

A. 36 years old

B. 40 years old

C. 44 years old

D. 48 years old

5.10 Name the only Olympic hockey team in 2006 that did not have a single active NHLer on its roster.

A. Team Kazakhstan

B. Team Italy

C. Team Latvia

D. Team Switzerland

5.11 Among goalies with NHL experience, what is the fewest number of NHL games played by a number one stopper at the 2006 Olympics?

A. Less than 20 NHL games
B. Between 20 and 50 games
C. Between 50 and 100 games
D. More than 100 games

5.12 Which coach was accused of tanking a game during the 2006 Olympics?

A. Canadian coach Pat Quinn
B. Russian coach Vladimir Krikunov
C. Swedish coach Bengt-Ake Gustafsson
D. Finnish coach Erkka Westerlund

5.13 What was the most penalty minutes handed out to a player in men's hockey at the 2006 Olympics?

A. 14 minutes
B. 20 minutes
C. 26 minutes
D. 32 minutes

5.14 Which NHLer participating in Torino, Italy, had the most career Olympic points after the Winter Games in 2006?

A. Chris Chelios of the USA
B. Teemu Selanne of Finland
C. Mats Sundin of Sweden
D. Robert Lang of the Czech Republic

5.15 Who was named MVP of the Olympic men's hockey tournament in 2006?

A. Peter Forsberg of Sweden
B. Daniel Alfredsson of Sweden
C. Saku Koivu of Finland
D. Antero Niittymaki of Finland

5.16 Which Swede couldn't participate in the official gold-medal celebration in Stockholm after the 2006 Olympics?

A. Nicklas Lidstrom
B. Fredrik Modin
C. Peter Forsberg
D. Mats Sundin

5.17 Who was the only member of *Sports Illustrated*'s All-Tournament team who didn't win a medal at the 2006 Olympics?

A. Alexander Ovechkin of Russia
B. Brad Richards of Canada
C. Marian Hossa of Slovakia
D. Pavel Datsyuk of Russia

5.18 Who is the only player in NHL history to have won a Stanley Cup, Olympic gold medal, World Championship, World Cup, Memorial Cup and World Junior Title?

A. Joe Sakic
B. Mario Lemieux
C. Scott Niedermayer
D. Steve Yzerman

Answers

5.1   **A. Sweden**
How Swede it was in the all-Nordic final of the 2006 Winter
Games. Winning the gold medal in a 3–2 showdown against
Finland, Sweden not only atoned for an Olympic-size embarrassment to Belarus in 2002 but avenged an early exit against
the Finns in 1998. Sweden's road to victory will be an object
lesson for many teams in future Olympic competition. After
three wins and a loss, the Swedes intentionally held back
against Slovakia in the final preliminary-round game to
draw the Swiss into the quarterfinals. That strategic 3–0 loss
to Slovakia and routine 6–2 win against Switzerland gave
Sweden the momentum to handily defeat the Czechs 7–3
in the semifinals. Meanwhile, Finland, the only undefeated
team in the competition, came into the finals running on
empty, despite a heady adrenaline rush. After the loss, Teemu
Selanne admitted his team had "heavy legs" and couldn't
keep up with Sweden's four lines, which kept making all-
important plays around the Finnish defense. Still, the Finns
scored the first goal and almost tied the game in a furious
rush in the dying moments, when Olli Jokinen had Henrik
Lundqvist beat and lunging to stop the puck with the fat part
of his goal stick. "I tried to go high," Jokinen said. "But it hit
his stick. It's a tough way to lose a game." Three key veterans—
Peter Forsberg, Mats Sundin and Nicklas Lidstrom—figured

in Sweden's winning goal, a stunning slap shot from Lidstrom near the blue line just 10 seconds into the third period.

5.2   C. 10 players

There were a few roster changes when teams finally took to the ice in Torino, but Colorado and Detroit still had the edge with 10 players each at the Olympics. The Avalanche's 10 Olympians (there were 11 until Ossi Vaananen broke his leg on February 2) were from more than eight countries, a tournament-high for one NHL club. The New York Rangers sent nine members to Italy, followed by Ottawa with eight. Chicago and Phoenix were each represented by just one player. Meanwhile, the Red Wings had the most NHLers on one Olympic team: five with Sweden. Finland dressed four Dallas Stars, and the Czech Republic, which iced players from the largest number of NHL teams, 16, included four Rangers. Canada had players from 15 NHL teams; Russia from 14 franchises.

5.3   A. The Tampa Bay Lightning

Between the Lightning and the Panthers, Florida teams contributed five players, or almost 22 per cent, to Canada's final roster, including Tampa Bay's Brad Richards, Martin St. Louis and Vincent Lacavalier; and Florida's Roberto Luongo and Jay Bouwmeester (who replaced the injured Scott Neidermayer). Players from every Canadian-based NHL club except Montreal were represented on Team Canada, and Ontario led all Canadian provinces with nine Olympians.

5.4   D. 13 players

Even though the USA had the oldest team in men's hockey at the 2006 Olympics, it still had 13 players making their first

Olympic appearance. The Americans brought a transition team to Torino with new bloods such as Scott Gomez, Craig Conroy, Brian Gionta and Rick DiPietro playing alongside a distinguished cast of veterans: Chris Chelios, Mike Modano, Bill Guerin, Keith Tkachuk and Doug Weight. Yet despite a big-name presence on the elite squad, Team USA could not overcome a lack of scoring, especially on the power play, dropping four straight one-goal games that included a 4–3 quarterfinal loss to silver-medalist Finland. The lack of practice time also worked against the Americans, who displayed little of the team play and self-confidence that won them the silver medal at the 2002 Games. Nine different states contributed players, five each from Michigan and New York, while one Canadian made Team USA: Toronto-born Mike Knuble, who was raised in Grand Rapids, Michigan. The American roster featured players from 13 NHL teams and only one Canadian franchise: Calgary Flames defenseman Jordon Leopold, from Golden Valley, Minnesota.

5.5   B. Russia

With all the talent of a $94-million team, how does Canada get shut out three times and fail to score a goal in 11 of its last 12 periods of Olympic play? It certainly wasn't the absence of youth or leadership, the off-ice distractions or the big ice that dashed Canada's hopes, but simply the failure to gel as a team. Scoring never materialized because there was no chemistry. And what about player selection? Hockey Canada promised to bring the best NHLers at the time. Sure, Sidney Crosby, but where was Eric Stall, the most dominating player before the Olympics? Still, Canada's final game against Russia was classic, a thrilling 2–0 nail-biter against its old rivals. But "we still were relying on our individual skills and we just didn't get over that hump that we needed to get over," admitted coach Pat Quinn.

5.6   C. Finland

Although the gold medal eluded Finland, it played a team game throughout the tournament, earning Saku Koivu and linemate Teemu Selanne the scoring lead (each with 11 points). The two players, along with Jere Lehtinen and Ollie Jokinen (with eight points between them), powered Finland's offense. Five of the top 10 point-earners were Finns.

Top Scorers at the 2006 Olympics

PLAYER	COUNTRY	GP	G	A	PTS	+/-	PIM
Teemu Selanne	Finland	8	6	5	11	7	4
Saku Koivu	Finland	8	3	8	11	5	12
Marian Hossa	Slovakia	6	5	5	10	9	4
Daniel Alfredsson	Sweden	8	5	5	10	2	4
Ville Peltonen	Finland	8	4	5	9	4	6

5.7   D. 46 goals scored; two goals allowed

There was some inevitability about the outcome in women's hockey at the 2006 Olympics. Canada, as defending champion, cruised to glory and another gold by dominating the opposition in all five games, including the final match against the tournament's biggest surprise, Sweden. Canada's women methodically demolished Italy 16–0, Russia 12–0 and Sweden 8–1 in the round robin, then set their sites on Finland with a 6–0 semifinals win and 4–1 victory against the Swedes to clinch the gold medal. The tally? Canada outscored its opposition 46–2 and outplayed them by a margin of 193 to 59 shots on goal. But the Canadians never once faced their arch-enemy, Team USA, as Sweden upset the Americans in a bold shootout victory that saw 19-year-old goaltender Kim Martin stop 37 of 39 shots and all four shootout attempts in a 3–2 semifinals win. It was considered the biggest upset of women's hockey, one that set the stage for the first ever championship finals not involving a USA–Canada showdown.

5.8   A. Team USA

For all the controversy over the age of Canada's Olympic team in 2006, it was the old guys who dominated not only the gold-medal game but also the top of the scoring charts. As well, three older and more experienced teams than Canada's advanced to the semifinals. Only the American greybeards proved the exception, finishing well out of medal contention. Among the six elite teams, Team Russia had the youngest roster at 27.9 years, followed by Team Canada's 29.4 years, Team Finland's 29.5 years, Team Sweden's 29.6 years, Team Czech Republic's 30.7 years and Team USA's 31.2 years.

5.9   D. 48 years old

When the U.S. Olympic team announced its 23-man roster for the 2006 Winter Games in Torino, 44-year-old defenseman Chris Chelios made the cut, becoming the third-oldest hockey player in Olympic history. After the announcement, an elated Chelios said, "If we have success, maybe they'll ask me back a fifth time." That would make the Detroit defenseman 48 years old at the 2010 Olympics in Vancouver and the same age as Hungarian Bela Ordody and German Alfred Steinka, the oldest hockey players in Olympic history. Ordody and Steinka competed at the age of 48 in the 1928 Olympics in St. Moritz. Unfortunately, Germany and Hungary finished 10th- and 11th-place overall during that tournament.

5.10 B. Team Italy

The host Italian team had nine Canadian-born and two U.S.-born players on its roster, but no active NHLers. Jason Cirone, Tony Tuzzolino and Jason Muzzatti were the only three with NHL experience. Among transplanted North Americans, Team Italy iced Canadian goalie Muzzatti, who had 62 NHL games behind him, and American Bob Nardella, who helped the IHL Chicago Wolves to two championships. Italy finished with only two points after three losses and two ties for 11th place in the 12-team tournament, a ranking just ahead of last-place Latvia with one active NHLer, Karlis Skrastins of Colorado.

5.11 A. Less than 20 NHL games

Not only did the Colorado Avalanche send the most NHLers to Torino, all three of its netminders saw Olympic action in 2006. Among the three (David Aebischer, Vitaliy Kolesnik and Peter Budaj), only Kolesnik played backup—to Vitaliy Veremeyev—for Kazakhstan. Aebischer, the most experienced NHLer of the group, led Switzerland. Budaj backstopped Slovakia with the tournament's lowest NHL game total for a number one man, 19 games. And even though Kolesnik had NHL experience (just seven games), he was number two behind Dynamo Moscow's Veremeyev, who had no NHL past. Other number one men with little NHL jam included Finland's Antero Niittymaki (37 games with Philadelphia) and Sweden's

Hedrik Lundqvist (40 games with the New York Rangers). All Olympic teams had some NHL presence between the pipes. Even Italy, without an active NHLer on the roster, had Jason Muzzatti, Calgary's 1988 first draft choice. Muzzatti had more than 60 NHL games to his credit—though none since 1997–98.

5.12   C. Swedish coach Bengt-Ake Gustafsson

Considering Sweden won gold, the strategy, if that's what it was, paid off handsomely. Did the Swedes intentionally lose a game to Slovakia in the round robin in order to duck the Czech Republic or Canada and play lowly Switzerland? *Before* the 3–0 loss to Slovakia, Bengt-Ake Gustafsson said, "It's difficult. As it looks right now, we will be facing Switzerland. But if we win we can get the Czechs or Canada. And, of course, it is the question: Shall we win or shall we play a good game to get a 0–0 result?" But after the IIHF expressed concern over his comments, Gustafsson backtracked, saying, "You've got to try to save your energy for the next game, which is the important one... That's all I said... Perhaps I said too much, I don't know." The powerhouse Swedes, who were outshot 31–17 by Slovakia, then went on to beat, in succession, Switzerland 6–2, the Czech Republic 7–3 and Finland 3–2 for the gold.

5.13   D. 32 minutes

It might seem like Italy wasn't playing the gracious host at its own Olympics, when the men's hockey team averaged a tournament-high of nearly 26 minutes per game and gritty forward Tony Tuzzolino collected a leading 32 penalty minutes in the box. But those numbers were spiked in Italy's fourth game of the preliminary round against the Czech

Republic on February 19. Tuzzolino's meltdown in the second period, after the Czechs made it 3–0 on a goal by Vaclav Prospal, earned the winger 30 minutes in box time (from a 10-minute misconduct and 20-minute abuse of official penalty). Three players—Finn Jarkko Ruutu and Olympic rookies Evgeni Malkin and Ilya Kovalchuk of Russia—recorded 31 minutes. The next top penalty men halved that total: Canada's Vincent Lacavalier and Mathieu Schneider of the usa each had 16 minutes.

5.14 B. Teemu Selanne of Finland

Winning the Olympic gold medal in 2006 would have been the cherry on Teemu Selanne's international career. It was his fourth and probably final Olympics. He even hinted that if Finland won the gold, he might give up international competition. At Torino, the 35-year-old Selanne suited up alongside Saku Koivu and Jere Lehtinen, a line that had played together internationally for a decade. He was revitalized and, as in 1998, shared the scoring lead again with Koivu. Yet despite their one-two finish, the Finns lost the gold medal to Sweden. Selanne, who won bronze in 1998 and the silver in 2006, will be almost 40 at the 2010 Games in Vancouver. If he retires, he retires as point-scoring leader, ahead of Koivu, with one less Olympic tournament.

The NHL's Top-Scoring Olympians*

PLAYER	COUNTRY	YEAR	GP	G	A	PTS
Teemu Selanne	Finland	1992	8	7	4	11
		1998	5	4	6	10**
		2002	4	3	0	3
		2006	8	6	5	11
		Total	25	20	15	35
Saku Koivu	Finland	1994	8	4	3	7
		1998	6	2	8	10**
		2006	8	3	8	11**
		Total	22	9	19	28
Robert Lang	Czechoslovakia	1992	8	5	8	13
	Czech Republic	1998	6	0	3	3
		2002	4	1	2	3
		2006	8	0	4	4
		Total	26	6	17	23

*Active NHLers in 2006 Olympics
**Olympic scoring leader

5.15 D. Antero Niittymaki of Finland

It's the only Olympic medal that gets no respect: the silver in men's hockey. Yet considering the silver-medal winners weren't even expected to make the quarterfinals and that they came without seven (yes, *seven*) key players, including number one goalie Miikka Kiprusoff, the under-the-radar Finns were nothing less than spectacular; just don't ask the silver medalists themselves. Following the game, Finnish sniper Olli Jokinen said, "You win bronze and gold, but you lose silver." After allowing only five goals in seven games, the near-perfect Finnish team gave up three to Sweden in the gold-medal game, one goal too many in a bitter 3–2 loss. The Finns made it to the finals with team play, superb penalty killing and bar-the-door goaltending from Antero Niittymaki, who was named tournament MVP for his 5–1–0 record, three shutouts and 1.34 GAA. Yes, it was only the silver, but an Olympic MVP title for a goalie in a backup role has to be some consolation.

5.16 B. Fredrik Modin

After their gold-medal win at the 2006 Olympics, Swedish players celebrated at a big party in Stockholm. The Detroit Red Wings excused five members of their team—Niklas Lidstrom, Henrik Zetterberg, Tomas Holmstrom, Mikael Samuelsson and Niklas Kronwall—to participate in the celebration, but countryman Fredrik Modin was asked to return to Tampa Bay to play against Florida. "If you ask me, I'm disappointed about not being able to celebrate with my country, absolutely," said Modin. But neither decision worked out for either team in their first games after the Olympic break. Modin's chance for a celebration was wasted, as the Lightning lost 8–2 to the Panthers; and Detroit, down five Swedes, was pounded 6–1 by San Jose. Still, Red Wing coach Mike Babcock was upbeat in their absence. "Are you going to tell them not to go to Sweden after they won the gold medal? There's not a chance in the world. They earned that."

5.17 A. Alexander Ovechkin of Russia

Sports Illustrated's Michael Farber named the 2006 Olympic's All-Tournament team, tapping three Finns, two Swedes and one Russian to *SI*'s elite roster. Farber said Finnish goalie Antero Niittymaki was "nearly impregnable until the final"; called Finn blueliner Kimmo Timonen "the best NHL defenseman nobody knows"; praised Swede rearguard Kenny Jonsson's return to form; picked Saku Koivu of Sweden over Mats Sundin at centre; anointed Daniel Alfredsson "the practically perfect player"; and wrote this about Alexander Ovechkin's five goals in six games: "Ovechkin isn't the best player since Bobby Orr, obviously—only the most exciting." Russia finished fourth after a 3–0 bronze-medal loss to the Czech Republic.

5.18   C. Scott Niedermayer

Imagine the size of Scott Niedermayer's rec room. His three commemorative Stanley Cups fill one corner, but then there is all that hardware from his international competitions. He is literally hockey's biggest winner—a title holder of all six of hockey's most prestigious championships. Besides his Stanley Cups in 1995, 2000 and 2003 with New Jersey, Niedermayer represented Canada and won Olympic gold in 2002, a World Championship and World Cup in 2004 and the World Junior Title in 1991. In 1991–92 he then made his NHL appearance in four of the Devils' first 22 games and was assigned to the WHL Kamloops Blazers, where he won the Memorial Cup in 1992. And as a measure of the international hockey community's regard for Niedermayer, when Canada flopped at the 2006 Olympics, Niedermayer's absence (due to injury) was one of the main factors cited behind that country's poor results in the tournament.

NHL Olympians

EVERY NHL TEAM CONTRIBUTED at least one player to the 2006 Olympics in Torino, Italy. Yet while some Olympic rosters featured lineups stocked solely with NHL talent, others such as Kazakhstan had just two active NHLers and host-nation Italy had none. In all, 151 players from the world's best pro league vied to be part of the world's best team. Match the 11 Olympic squads on the right with the active NHLer in the left column they showcased.

Solutions are on page 122

1. _____	Toronto's Nik Antropov	A. Team Finland
2. _____	Nashville's Tomas Vokoun	B. Team Russia
3. _____	Vancouver's Todd Bertuzzi	C. Team Germany
4. _____	Washington's Olaf Kolzig	D. Team USA
5. _____	Florida's Olli Jokinen	E. Team Sweden
6. _____	Ottawa's Zdeno Chara	F. Team Canada
7. _____	Colorado's Karlis Strastins	G. Team Slovakia
8. _____	Detroit's Pavel Datysyuk	H. Team Latvia
9. _____	Tampa Bay's Fredrik Modin	I. Team Switzerland
10. _____	Montreal's Mark Streit	J. Team Kazakhstan
11. _____	Buffalo's Chris Drury	K. Team Czech Republic

6

Team Dreams

WHEN HE WAS GROWING UP, Sidney Crosby's favourite players were Wayne Gretzky, Steve Yzerman and Mario Lemieux, though the team he dreamed of playing for was the Montreal Canadiens. That fantasy didn't materialize, but Crosby's first NHL game against Montreal on November 10, 2005, did have a fairy tale ending. The 18-year-old sensation scored the first goal of the contest, then later notched the game-winner as his Penguins posted a 3–2 shootout victory on home ice. After teammates Mark Recchi and Mario Lemieux were denied by Canadiens goalie José Théodore, Crosby skated in, faked Théodore to his knees and roofed a backhand into the top of the net, sending the netminder's water bottle skyward and the Mellon Arena crowd into a frenzy. "It's so amazing, it's hard to believe," Crosby said later. "I was just fortunate to get that shot. I got lucky with that shot."

Answers are on page 92

6.1 Which NHL club celebrated a victory in 2005–06 by sending their entire team on the ice when the first star was announced after the game?

A. The Vancouver Canucks

B. The Buffalo Sabres

C. The New York Rangers

D. The Atlanta Thrashers

6.2 **Which NHL team served up the "Pizza Line" in 2005–06?**

A. The San Jose Sharks

B. The Colorado Avalanche

C. The Philadelphia Flyers

D. The Ottawa Senators

6.3 **With what team and league did Carolina sniper Eric Stall lose his first tooth playing hockey?**

A. Playing with the Peterborough Petes in the OHL

B. Playing with the Lowell Lock Monsters in the AHL

C. Playing with the Carolina Hurricanes in the NHL

D. Stall has never broken any teeth

6.4 **Which NHL team has the best winning-percentage in season openers?**

A. The Colorado Avalanche

B. The New Jersey Devils

C. The Buffalo Sabres

D. The Montreal Canadiens

6.5 **Which Central Hockey League team made history in 2005 by icing pro hockey's first brother-sister duo?**

A. The Austin Ice Bats

B. The Wichita Thunder

C. The Tulsa Oilers

D. The Odessa Jackalopes

6.6 **Which team recorded the NHL's first win by shootout?**

A. The Toronto Maple Leafs

B. The Ottawa Senators

C. The Pittsburgh Penguins

D. The Calgary Flames

6.7 **What 2005–06 story was hockey analyst Glenn Healy talking about when he said, "I got to buy some of those drugs that Boston's been smoking"?**

A. The 2006 Winter Olympics in Torino, Italy

B. The Joe Thornton trade

C. The firing of Bruin general manager Mike O'Connell

D. The NHL's new substance abuse program

6.8 **What is the minimum age for playing on an Ottawa seniors team called the Geriatric Buzzards?**

A. 40 years old

B. 50 years old

C. 60 years old

D. 70 years old

6.9 **What is the most points recorded by an NHL team on a road trip?**

A. 13 points

B. 15 points

C. 17 points

D. 19 points

6.10 **In 2003–04, how many home games did Pittsburgh lose, establishing a new NHL record for ineptitude?**

A. 13 games

B. 14 games

C. 15 games

D. 16 games

6.11 The Pittsburgh Penguins snapped an NHL-record, 14-game home losing streak on a tying goal by defenseman Marc Bergevin in 2003–04. How long had it been since Bergevin last scored a goal?

A. 42 games

B. 62 games

C. 82 games

D. 102 games

6.12 Even though Pittsburgh lost more games in a row (home and away) in 2003–04 than any other team in NHL history, the streak is not a league record. Why?

A. One of the losses was in overtime

B. One of the losses was a postponed game

C. One of the losses was a neutral-site game

D. There is no official NHL record for most consecutive losses

6.13 Which is the first pro hockey team to win 50 or more games in five successive seasons?

A. The Houston Aeros of the AHL

B. The Quad City Mallards of the UHL

C. The Tulsa Oilers of the CHL

D. The Hersey Bears of the AHL

6.14 What NHL team in 2005–06 set a regular-season record for most wins when trailing after 40 minutes?

A. The Colorado Avalanche

B. The New York Rangers

C. The Dallas Stars

D. The Toronto Maple Leafs

6.15 **What famous event in Montreal Canadiens history took place on March 11?**

A. The legendary Howie Morenz was honoured with a rare funeral service at the Montreal Forum

B. The Canadiens played their last game at the Montreal Forum

C. The death and sweater retirement of Hall of Famer Bernie Geoffrion

D. All of the above

6.16 **Several successful NHL teams iced rosters with multiple Europeans in 2005–06. What was the most players from one European country on an NHL team that season?**

A. Five Europeans from one country

B. Six Europeans from one country

C. Seven Europeans from one country

D. Eight Europeans from one country

6.17 **In 2005–06, the first true season of zero-tolerance policy on obstruction, teams enjoyed how many power plays compared to the previous season, 2003–04, when there were a league-wide 10,427 power-play opportunities?**

A. There were fewer; between 8,000 and 10,000 power plays

B. The same; between 10,000 and 11,000 power plays

C. There were more; between 11,000 and 13,000 power plays

D. There were more than 13,000 power plays

6.18 **Which NHL team record did the Detroit Red Wings break in 2005–06?**

A. Most wins in one season

B. Most road wins in one season

C. Fewest losses in one season

D. Most road losses in one season

Answers

6.1   **B. The Buffalo Sabres**

It's the kind of team spirit that coaches kill for. After stressing production in even-strength situations, Buffalo coach Lindy Ruff saw his Sabres annihilate the Los Angeles Kings 10–1 on January 14, 2006, with six even-strength goals, three more on the power play and another on a shorthanded breakaway. "Pretty well everyone chipped in," said Ruff. "It was a great team effort from top to bottom. The forward lines did a lot of work down low, controlled play, cycled the puck and got rewarded for it." Rookie forward Jason Pominville—with a natural hat trick—and Jochen Hecht scored three goals apiece. "It's awesome," said Pominville. "It doesn't happen too often. So it's fun to see the team work hard and have it finally pay off." Twelve Sabres earned 27 individual points, while Chris Drury got the third star and Pominville the second. Then, when Hecht was named the game's first star, the entire team skated onto the ice. "It was a good night for everybody on our team," said Hecht. "Everybody played hard, and everybody deserved the first star."

6.2   **D. The Ottawa Senators**

When the Senators line of Daniel Alfredsson, Jason Spezza and Dany Heatley began running roughshod over the opposition early in the 2005–06 season, the *Ottawa Citizen* ran a contest to find a name for the high-powered trio. Unfortunately, the winning entry, the Cash Line, generated little enthusiasm.

Instead, many people referred to the trio as the Pizza Line. For several years, the pizza chain Pizza Pizza had been running a promotion in which it awarded a free slice of pie to every fan with a ticket stub for an Ottawa home victory in which the team scored five or more goals. Prior to 2005–06, the low-scoring Senators were no threat to Pizza Pizza's ovens. However, in 2005–06, the Sens reached the magic number five in the first three games. Fearing a loss of dough, in the literal sense, Pizza Pizza changed its slice standard to six goals. But with Alfredsson, Spezza and Heatley lighting the lamp, the team hit the six-goal mark six times in its first 19 home games, filling fans' stomachs and giving Pizza Pizza a steady dose of acid indigestion.

6.3   C. Playing with the Carolina Hurricanes in the NHL

During a lifetime of playing with sticks and pucks, Stall defied the odds: he never lost a tooth in action. Then, in a game against St. Louis on January 15, 2006, the Hurricanes forward was initiated into hockey's rudimentary form of tooth extraction following a high stick from the Blues' Dennis Wideman that cut Stall's lip (requiring several stitches) and chipped half of one of his incisors. "I've got a lot of chin scars, but I never lost a tooth," said Stall, who scored a hat trick in the 4–2 come-from-behind win.

6.4   A. The Colorado Avalanche

After a 4–3 loss to Edmonton in 2005–06's season opener on October 5, new Colorado defenseman Patrice Brisebois said the Avalanche skated with "two feet in the sand." Joe Sakic opinioned, "81 more to go." It may be just another game, but the loss didn't hurt Colorado, the league leader in season openers.

Highest/Lowest Win-Percentages in Season Openers*

TEAM	GP	W	L	T	PCT.	GF	GA
Colorado	26	15	5	6	.692	104	71
New Jersey	31	17	7	7	.661	113	91
Ottawa	13	6	2	5	.654	44	36
Montreal	88	47	26	15	.619	303	219
Carolina	26	6	15	5	.326	67	94
Columbus	5	1	3	1	.300	11	14
Anaheim	12	3	9	0	.250	24	38
San Jose	14	2	10	2	.214	38	54

*Including 2005–06

6.5   C. The Tulsa Oilers

On January 28, 2005, Angela Ruggiero became the first
female non-goaltender to play in a U.S. men's professional
hockey game, when she laced them up for the Tulsa Oilers
in a Central Hockey League tilt against the Rio Grande
Valley Killer Bees. Making the occasion doubly memorable,
Ruggiero's brother, Bill, was the Oilers' goaltender. Together,
the Ruggieros became the first brother-and-sister pairing to
play in a North American professional game. "It was all that
I could ask for," said the 25-year-old rearguard after Tulsa's
7–2 victory over the Killer Bees. Ruggiero, who won gold, silver and bronze as a member of the 1998, 2002 and 2006 U.S.
Women's Olympic teams, played 13 shifts that totalled 13:05,
recorded an assist on the game's final goal, finished plus-two
and did not shy away from physical contact. Seconds after
being checked in her third shift of the game, she answered

with a hit of her own by knocking a Killer Bees player into the boards. "I'm used to getting hit," said Ruggiero. "There was definitely a lot of contact, but it was all clean. That's hockey. It's a rough game."

6.6 B. The Ottawa Senators

The first shootout win in NHL history went to Ottawa on the first night of NHL play in 2005–06. With Toronto 2–2 and 1:02 remaining in regulation time, Daniel Alfredsson scored to tie the game. Then, after a scoreless five-minute overtime, the Ottawa captain connected again on the Senators' first attempt under the new shootout format to settle tied games. The Leafs' Jason Allison and Eric Lindros failed in their efforts against Dominik Hasek, but Dany Heatley scored on Ottawa's third chance, clinching the win with two points for the Senators. Toronto coach Pat Quinn, no fan of the shootout, was diplomatic after the outcome, saying "I'm not one of the ones that like the game being settled this way." The Leafs' Ed Belfour is the first netminder in NHL history to suffer a shoot-out loss. Heatley and Alfredsson's sticks were subsequently sent to the Hockey Hall of Fame.

6.7 B. The Joe Thornton trade

The deal stunned everyone. First, because it was Joe Thornton, the face of the Boston franchise. Then, because Boston's star captain had just signed a three-year contract worth U.S.$20 million. And finally, because of what the Bruins received in return. Frankly, it looked like a bag of pucks. But Wayne Primeau, Marco Strum and Brad Stuart injected life into the underachieving Bruins as the season progressed. Still, in 532 career games, Thornton had 454 points, just 108 fewer than the combined totals of Primeau, Strum and Stuart, who played in 918 more games than the hulking forward centre. The deal had Glenn Healy wondering what herb the Bruins' executives were ingesting to make them believe dealing Thornton was a good idea. It wasn't, and, late in the season, Boston general manager Mike O'Connell was fired.

6.8   D. 70 years old

It's the ultimate hockey comeback. To play with the Geriatric Senior Buzzards you have to be skilled, dedicated, fearless and, yes, at least 70 years old—or battling serious ailments such as cancer or heart problems. Mario Lemieux and all his health issues have nothing on these guys. In 2005–06, the 22-man lineup featured Norm Sauliner, 70 (and fighting prostrate cancer); Wayne Currie, 66 (triple bypass survivor); and Ron Davis, 69 (knee with steel plate). To a man, the Buzzards just want another go at the sport they've played their entire lives—despite the health risks and concerns of loved ones. Their rule book advises: "Several of our players have had major surgery or have problems with their balance. Please be careful not to touch them when skating close to them." Yet it's a marvel to see the Buzzards play: a slow and deliberate game with sudden bursts of speed and competitive zeal. "We don't count goals," said team founder Jim Sullivan in a 2006 *National Post* story. "We count survival. We just want to live to play again."

6.9   C. 17 points

The Philadelphia Flyers were road warriors during a gruelling three-week, 11-game marathon in 2005–06, notching an impressive 8–2–0–1 record to claim honours for the most productive road trip in NHL history. No team in league annals has come home with 17 points. But NHL schedulers take note: The Flyers' tank was running on empty. Philadelphia lost two of its last three away games and its return to the Wachovia Center was a disaster, with the club dropping its first three home games and losing in overtime to Colorado, in a shootout to Carolina and in regulation time to Boston. Philadelphia's 11-game swing matched the longest trip in modern NHL history. Eighteen years earlier, the Calgary Flames played 11 consecutive games away from the Saddledome when, in February 1988, the Winter Olympics came to town. But they didn't fare as well, going 5–5–1 for 11 points.

6.10   B. 14 games

If teams hung banners from the rafters for their NHL records, as they do for their championships, Pittsburgh's Igloo would be festooned with some doozies. Next to the banner celebrating the league's longest winning streak of 17 games in 1992–93, fans could be reminded of the Penguins' embarrassing 14-game home losing streak in 2003–04—the longest in NHL history. The moribund Penguins took losing to new depths by bettering the four previous record-holding teams (with 11 straight defeats) by three losses. To add salt to Pittsburgh's wound, the four clubs—Boston, Washington, Ottawa and Atlanta—all suffered their slide as first-year expansion clubs. The December 31 to February 22 skid was on course to set another league mark for futility at home—the longest home winless streak. But the Penguins won on March 6 and halted their fall at 16 games, one short of the record 17 winless games held by Ottawa and Atlanta.

6.11   D. 102 games

You know your team is in deep trouble when it needs a goal from Marc Bergevin. The veteran blueliner notched just his 36th goal in 1,181 career games to snap Pittsburgh's 14-game home losing streak on March 2, 2004. Bergevin's weak wrist shot from the point fluttered past the Islanders' Garth Snow at 1:46 of the third period for the 3–3 tie with New York. "I saw the replay—it was a laser beam," joked Bergevin of his first goal in precisely 102 games. Bergevin hadn't scored since November 23, 2002.

6.12   A. One of the losses was in overtime

No one has talked to the Washington Capitals or the San Jose Sharks about Pittsburgh's 18-game losing streak in 2003–04, but they are probably not happy with the St. Louis Blues. In a losing stretch that could have changed the NHL record books and displaced Washington and San Jose from the top spot for most consecutive losses with 17, one of the Penguin's 18 defeats was in overtime, a 3–2 loss to St. Louis on February 14. Had the Blues beat the hapless Penguins in regulation time, hockey's losingest team would be Pittsburgh. Instead, their official record is 0–17–0–1, and the Capitals and Sharks remain the beacons of incompetence.

6.13   B. The Quad City Mallards of the UHL

It's a record unmatched by any other team in professional hockey history. In March 2001, the United Hockey League's Quad City Mallards, based in Moline, Illinois, completed their "Drive of Five" with five consecutive seasons of 50 or more regular-season wins—and that's in a 74-game schedule. With three Colonial Cups in that span, the Mallards are something of a success at rewriting the record books, both on and off the ice. In 2002 and again in 2004, the Iowa–Illinois border team collected its 50th wins for an unprecedented sixth and seventh time in eight years. The Mallards set UHL records for total season and average attendances and, in just their eighth season, almost hit the three-million mark in all-time attendance. As a result, all Quad City season ticket-holders were rewarded with free tickets to home playoff games as well as a "Legends Bobblehead Series," a limited-edition five-bobblehead set. The Mallards are among the first in pro hockey to broadcast all of their games live over the Internet. In February 2004, Cam Severson became the first former Mallard to score a point in the NHL while playing with the Anaheim Mighty Ducks.

6.14   C. The Dallas Stars

Mike Modano nailed it when he said, "We just keep finding ways to dig ourselves out of holes." In fact, the 2005–06 Dallas Stars were regular-season backhoes when entering the third period behind, first tying the NHL record with their ninth come-from-behind victory in a 2–1 win against Vancouver on March 11, then breaking the benchmark held by both the 2001–02 Toronto Maple Leafs and 2002–03 Boston Bruins, with a 4–3 win against San Jose on March 18, 2006. "I think all nine of them have been different, whether it's getting bombed early and me getting pulled or a tight game like [Saturday's]," goalie Marty Turco told the *Dallas Morning News* after the March 11 win. The Stars' record-setting 10th win when trailing after 40 minutes was won in a shootout and without the help of Jussi Jokinen, who surprisingly missed his attempt after converting his first nine shootout chances. Four of the record 10 comeback wins were by shootout, which only debuted in 2005–06. Dallas also maintained a perfect record with an NHL-best 10–0 in shootouts. (The record for most wins by a team trailing after 40 minutes is unofficial and probably only dates back to the 1990s.)

6.15 D. All of the above

Few dates hold as much significance in the storied history of the Club de Hockey Canadien as March 11. On that date, Montreal fans pay tribute to several events—most recently, the passing away of Bernie "Boom-Boom" Geoffrion on March 11, 2006. Just hours after Geoffrion's death from stomach cancer in an Atlanta hospice, the Canadiens retired his famous No. 5 in an emotional 40-minute banner-raising ceremony at centre ice of the Bell Centre. In attendance was the Geoffrion family, including wife Marlene, daughter of the great 1930s star Howie Morenz. In the last moments of his life, the Boomer insisted that everyone be there for his sweater retirement, when his banner would be raised next to Morenz's retired No. 7. "The first time dad took my mom on a date, he took her to a boxing match at the Forum," said Danny Geoffrion. "He told her that, one day, his sweater would hang up there next to her father's. Today, he kept that promise." Long criticized for not retiring several jersey numbers of past greats, the Canadiens finally scheduled the Geoffrion celebration for March 11 to coincide with the 10th anniversary of the last Habs game at the Forum, where Geoffrion starred for 14 years. It was also 69 years to the day after 12,500 fans attended funeral services at the Forum for his father-in-law, Howie Morenz. As well, the Canadiens were playing the New York Rangers, a team Geoffrion played for and coached after his career ended in Montreal. In the 1–0 Montreal win, Craig Rivet, fittingly, scored on a slap shot, the shot Geoffrion popularized and the inspiration for his famous nickname.

6.16 C. Seven Europeans from one country

Not since Scotty Bowman successfully united the Russian Five of Igor Larionov, Vladimir Konstantinov, Slava Fetisov, Slava Kozlov and Sergei Fedorov on the Detroit Red Wings have NHL teams been so Euro-centric as in 2005–06. European players have a home on every NHL roster, but the New York Rangers, Detroit Red Wings and Dallas Stars took Bowman's original plan to heart and injected their lineup with as many as seven regulars from one European country. Although some have called them the Czech Rangers, Swedish Red Wings and Finnish Stars, "It's not a master plan," said Detroit general manager Ken Holland in a *USA Today* interview. "We never said we want to get seven Swedes, but when we got four or five and they played well, you start to think, If you grow up playing a similar style of hockey, you might have pretty good on-ice chemistry."

Teams with Most Europeans from One Country in 2005–06

TEAM	COUNTRY	NO. OF PLAYERS
Detroit	Sweden	7—Nicklas Lidstrom, Henrik Zetterberg, Tomas Holmstrom, Mikael Samuelsson, Niklas Kronwall, Andreas Lilja and Johan Franzen
NYR	Czech R.	7—Jaromir Jagr, Martin Straka, Martin Rucinsky, Petr Sykora, Petr Prucha, Marek Malik and Michal Rozsival
Dallas	Finland	6—Jere Lehtinen, Jussi Jokinen, Niko Kapanen, Antti Miettinen, Niklas Hagman and Janne Niinimaa

6.17 D. There were more than 13,000 power plays

When Stephen Walkom was appointed as the NHL's new director of officiating in August 2005, his directive was ice clear: Stop all the hooking, holding and crosschecking by bringing in a consistent standard of rule enforcement for the entire season. That didn't mean no contact, it meant no fouling in the bump-and-grind play. And, if goals and power-play stats are any indication, Walkom realized his mandate: The crackdown on obstruction created more offense and more offensive opportunities in 2005–06. Here are a few numbers to bang around. Goal scoring was up 18 per cent, or one goal per game, from a five-year low of 5.1 goals per game in 2003–04 to 6.1 in 2005–06—the largest percentage increase since 1929–30. As well, there were 10,427 power plays in 2003–04 and 14,390 in 2005–06, a whopping leap of 28 per cent thanks to Walkom and the NHL's zero-tolerance policy. This led to 2,545 power-play goals—826 more than in 2003–04, when 1,717 were scored on the man-advantage.

6.18 B. Most road wins in one season

One of the teams expected to be hit hardest by the NHL's new economic structure in 2005–06 was Detroit. But the free-spending Red Wings showed surprising resiliency under the league's U.S.$39-million salary cap. Defenseman Mathieu Schneider may have had the best answer when he said, "I think the reality is, guys really want to play here." As a result, the Red Wings kept many core players, including Pavel Datsyuk, Brendan Shanahan, Henrik Zetterberg, Nicklas Lidstrom and Manny Legace, who netted an NHL-record 10 wins in October to hand Detroit an early lead in the Western Conference. Another key to success was coach

Mike Babcock, who kept his club poised against third-period comebacks with his "Keep your foot on the gas, just keep playing" philosophy to avoid falling into a defensive shell. As a result, Detroit scored more goals in the third period (107) than any other frame, finished second behind Ottawa in total shots (2,796) and out-shot opponents a league-high 62 times in 82 games. The Wings also became the all-time-best road warriors, tying New Jersey's 28-win mark in 1998–99 on April 3 with a 2–1 shootout win against Calgary and then setting a new high of 31 victories on the road to cap 2005–06.

Chris Who?

FOR EVERY VINCENT LECAVALIER of Tampa Bay or Martin Brodeur of New Jersey, there are dozens of champions like Chris Dingman, who win the Stanley Cup but rarely get the ink or air time of their high-profile teammates. In this game, all of the Cup-winners in the left column played with their respective championship clubs for the majority of the regular and postseason, including Dingman with his two-Cup performances in 2001 and 2004. Try to match them with their Cup-winning teams on the right.

Solutions are on page 122

PART 1

1. _____ Chris Dingman	A. Edmonton Oilers, 1988
2. _____ Jiri Fischer	B. Pittsburgh Penguins, 1992
3. _____ Kevin Haller	C. Tampa Bay Lightning, 2004
4. _____ Hector Marini	D. New York Islanders, 1982
5. _____ Troy Loney	E. Detroit Red Wings, 2002
6. _____ Craig Muni	F. Montreal Canadiens, 1993

PART 2

1. _____ Colin Patterson	A. Colorado Avalanche, 2001
2. _____ Ace Bailey	B. Boston Bruins, 1972
3. _____ Dave Reid	C. New York Rangers, 1994
4. _____ Jay Pandolfo	D. Calgary Flames, 1989
5. _____ Dan Hinote	E. Dallas Stars, 1999
6. _____ Brian Noonan	F. New Jersey Devils, 2003

7

The **B**ig Dance

IT'S NOT OFTEN that a son follows in the footsteps of his *mother* to become a Stanley Cup winner, but that's exactly what John Grahame did to win the Cup as Nikolai Khabibulin's backup on the Tampa Bay Lightning in 2004. Grahame's mother, Charlotte, one of only eight women to have their name on the Cup, was Colorado's director of hockey operations when the Avalanche won the Cup in 2001.

Answers are on page 109

7.1 **In which NHL city is the Red Mile?**
- A. Detroit
- B. Calgary
- C. Nashville
- D. San Jose

7.2 **Who are the Wednesday Nighters?**
- A. An Edmonton beer league featuring ex-NHL tough guys
- B. A barn-storming team of former NHL stars
- C. A checking line with the Boston Bruins
- D. A pick-up league famous for challenging the NHL's control of the Stanley Cup

7.3 Which NHL goaltending record did Miikka Kiprusoff set during the 2004 playoffs?

A. Most minutes played in one postseason
B. Most shots faced in one postseason
C. Most shutouts in one postseason
D. Most losses in one postseason

7.4 What is the NHL record for the most series-deciding overtime goals in a career?

A. Two overtime goals
B. Three overtime goals
C. Four overtime goals
D. Five overtime goals

7.5 In which NHL city did airport agents "lose" the Stanley Cup in August 2004?

A. Calgary
B. Tampa Bay
C. Vancouver
D. Chicago

7.6 Which NHL game generated the largest audience on CBC's *Hockey Night in Canada*?

A. Toronto vs. Los Angeles, Game 7, 1993, third round
B. Vancouver vs. New York, Game 7, 1994, finals
C. Toronto vs. Ottawa, Game 7, 2002, second round
D. Calgary vs. Tampa Bay, Game 7, 2004, finals

7.7 What is the longest span between Stanley Cup wins for a coach?

A. Nine years
B. 11 years

C. 13 years

D. 15 years

7.8   **What is the longest span between the first and last time an individual had his name engraved on the Stanley Cup?**

A. 23 years

B. 33 years

C. 43 years

D. 53 years

7.9   **What is the age of the oldest individual on the Stanley Cup?**

A. 67 years old

B. 77 years old

C. 87 years old

D. 97 years old

7.10   **What is the longest span between the first and last Stanley Cup wins by a player?**

A. 15 years

B. 17 years

C. 19 years

D. 21 years

7.11   **Which NHLer has played in the most Stanley Cup finals games without winning the Cup?**

A. Brad Park

B. Bruce MacGregor

C. Brian Propp

D. Dale Hunter

7.12   Prior to the Tampa Bay Lightning in 2004, when was
        the last time a team beat the Montreal Canadiens in
        the rounds before the finals and went on to win the
        Stanley Cup?
        A. In the 1964 playoffs
        B. In the 1974 playoffs
        C. In the 1984 playoffs
        D. In the 1994 playoffs

7.13   Which NHL club rewards its team's hardest-working player
        with a hard hat?
        A. The Boston Bruins
        B. The Calgary Flames
        C. The New Jersey Devils
        D. The Edmonton Oilers

7.14   What is the NHL record for most shutouts by a goalie in
        one playoff year?
        A. Five shutouts
        B. Six shutouts
        C. Seven shutouts
        D. Eight shutouts

7.15   Which NHLer set a new playoff record for game-winning
        goals after Joe Nieuwendyk tied Joe Sakic's record of six
        in 1999?
        A. Brett Hull of the Dallas Stars (in 2000)
        B. Peter Forsberg of the Colorado Avalanche (in 2002)
        C. Jamie Langebrunner of the New Jersey Devils (in 2003)
        D. Brad Richards of the Tampa Bay Lightning (in 2004)

7.16 Prior to 2005–06, which Stanley Cup finalist was the last to avenge its Cup loss by winning the championship the following year?

A. The Edmonton Oilers

B. The Calgary Flames

C. The Colorado Avalanche

D. The New Jersey Devils

7.17 How did ex-NHL coach Jacques Demers come to own the last hockey stick used by Wayne Gretzky in a Stanley Cup game?

A. He purchased it at an auction

B. He found it in an empty locker

C. He traded it for his Stanley Cup ring

D. He asked Gretzky himself for it

7.18 Including playoff goals, how many more goals than Gordie Howe did Wayne Gretzky compile as a professional?

A. Only one goal

B. Nine goals, the same number as Howe's sweater number

C. 72 goals, the same year number—1972—of Howe and Gretzky's first meeting

D. 99 goals, the same as Gretzky's sweater number

The Big Dance

Answers

7.1 **B. Calgary**

During the Flames' amazing 26-game run at the Stanley Cup in 2004, a four-block area west of the Saddledome was dubbed the Red Mile. Thousands of Calgary fans, thirsting for a Cup and sporting their team's scarlet jersey, flooded into the strip of bars, pubs and cafés to watch the big screen TVs and celebrate. Cars with horns blaring and festooned with Flames pennants cruised along 17th Avenue amidst throngs of fans and thunderous, fist-pumping cheers of "Go Flames Go." It was Calgary's first playoff series in seven seasons. But it all ended in heartbreak when Tampa Bay doused the Flames and their fans' celebratory mood with a 2–1 win in Game 7 of the finals.

7.2 D. A pick-up league famous for challenging the NHL's control of the Stanley Cup

The tradition of the Stanley Cup as a challenge trophy was given new life in February 2006 when the NHL reached an out-of-court settlement with Gard Shelley and David Burt, two Toronto-area recreational players who filed a court case to undermine the league's claim that it controlled the Cup. But beer leaguers' hopes of hoisting hockey's most famous trophy won't be realized any time soon. The agreement stipulates that the Cup trustees can award it to a team outside the NHL in a season when the league doesn't operate (which could be years away given the new CBA agreement) but that the trustees are under no obligation to award the Cup to just any challengers. "Our guys weren't going… to court to say the Wednesday Nighters group of geriatric hockey players deserve to have their name on the Cup," said Tim Gilbert, lead counsel for Shelley and Burt, in a *National Post* story. "It was that the Cup is bigger than the NHL." The pact also included a provision for the NHL to contribute $100,000 a year for five years to leagues for women and underprivileged children.

7.3   **A. Most minutes played in one postseason**

The trade that sent Miikka Kiprusoff from San Jose to Calgary on November 16, 2003, was the spark that the struggling Flames needed to make the playoffs for the first time in seven years. Thanks to the Finnish-born netminder's heroics, Calgary upset Vancouver and Detroit and advanced to the 2004 Stanley Cup finals before losing to Tampa Bay in seven games. Along the way, Kiprusoff set a new NHL record by playing 1,655 minutes in 26 postseason games, breaking the former mark of 1,544 minutes jointly held by Ed Belfour and Kirk McLean. Kiprusoff finished the 2004 playoffs with 15 wins and 11 losses, a 1.86 GAA and five shutouts.

7.4   **B. Three overtime goals**

Had Martin Gelinas lived 100 years ago he might have been a hired gun in the Old West. Before signing with Florida in 2005, he played on Stanley Cup finalists with every team that sought his services, except Quebec. Based on his postseason record with Edmonton, Vancouver, Carolina and Calgary, one could argue Gelinas is the ultimate playoff triggerman, a reliable third-liner who provides momentum-changing shifts with his energy and work ethic, a role player able to grind it out or fill in on better lines in case of injuries. Gelinas notched final appearances with the Stanley Cup-winning Oilers in 1990, the Canucks in 1994, the Hurricanes in 2002 and the Flames in 2004. But his one Cup aside, it is what he did in 2002 and 2004 that shines on his resumé. Gelinas took Carolina to the finals after knocking off Toronto with his Conference finals winner in overtime. Then, in 2004, Calgary eliminated Vancouver in the first round and Detroit in the second thanks to overtime winners by Gelinas. He is the first and only NHLer to end three playoff series with overtime goals.

7.5   C. Vancouver

So how does hockey's most revered trophy go missing? If you ask Air Canada officials in Vancouver, they would say the Stanley Cup was never actually lost or misplaced on their jet destined for Fort St. John, B.C., in August 2004. Apparently, the 35-pound (16-kg) Cup was booted from a full plane in Vancouver because of weight restrictions. But no one told Cup handler Walter Neubrand, who went into a tailspin after arriving in Fort St. John without it. Each summer, Lord Stanley's prize travels with members of the Stanley Cup winners, and it was Tampa Bay head scout Jake Goertzen's turn. After many anxious hours and a few cancelled showings of the Cup, a red-faced airline spokesperson confirmed that the "the Cup was held in a secure facility overnight. We always knew where it was." Truly lame.

7.6   B. Vancouver vs. New York, Game 7, 1994, finals

The United States and Canada might share the same NHL game on ice, but on television, the product is treated quite differently by the two countries. In 2004, NHL commissioner Gary Bettman had to settle for a revenue-sharing agreement with NBC, which meant no rights revenue for the league or any money up front. One factor was the slide in ABC's ratings during its five-year deal with the league. The network's numbers slumped from 3.7 (about 3.7 million households) in the 2000 finals to 2.6 in the 2004 finals. In Canada, with a population one-tenth that of the U.S., CBC averaged 2.15 million viewers for each telecast of the 2004 playoffs. Not surprisingly, Game 7 between Calgary and Tampa Bay drew the best numbers,

4.86 million. But that didn't surpass Vancouver–New York's Game 7 total in 1994, which attracted 4.95 million viewers, an all-time record for *Hockey Night in Canada.*

7.7   C. 13 years

After winning multiple Stanley Cups with Montreal, his last in 1979, Scotty Bowman was squeezed out of the organization in a front-office power play that left him bitter and determined to find another NHL job. It came in Buffalo. After seven seasons with the Sabres, Bowman quit coaching and only returned in 1991–92 to lead Pittsburgh to its second straight championship. It had been 13 years since his last Cup victory in 1979. Dick Irvin knew drought better than most coaches, winning only four of 16 Cup finals. His longest stretch was 12 years between Cups: Toronto in 1932 and Montreal in 1944.

7.8   D. 53 years

Marcel Pronovost has had a long and rewarding association with the game. He won five Stanley Cups as a hard-hitting defenseman with Detroit and Toronto, beginning in 1950, when he was called up during the playoffs to replace Red Kelly on the Red Wings blue line. Detroit won the Stanley Cup and Pronovost's name was etched in silver without him playing a single regular-season game. During his career, Pronovost never took home any individual awards, though he was named to All-Star teams on four occasions. After retiring in 1970, he coached junior hockey and scouted for the NHL's Central Scouting Bureau. Then, he landed a scouting job with New Jersey and saw his name on the Cup three more times when the Devils won championships in 1995, 2000 and 2003, more than a half-century after Pronovost's first Cup celebration.

7.9 **C. 87 years old**

The oldest player to win the Stanley Cup is Toronto's Johnny Bower, at age 42. The oldest person to get his name on the Cup is Wally Crossman, who worked in the Detroit dressing room for half a century—dating back to the early years of the Olympia. Crossman was a rink rat and hung around the old arena so much that the Red Wings offered him a job as stick boy. His name is on the Cup four times between 1951 and 1998, the last time as dressing room assistant, when he was age 87.

7.10 **D. 21 years**

Few playoff champions can rival the heroics of New York coach Lester Patrick. It was Patrick who famously strapped on the blood- and sweat-stained pads of injured Ranger goalie Lorne Chabot during the 1928 Cup finals. After losing Chabot to an eye injury midway through Game 2, the 44-year-old Patrick took over between the pipes and stopped all but one shot through two periods and a sudden-death overtime. The Rangers won 2–1 and eventually defeated the Montreal Maroons for their first Stanley Cup in franchise history. Patrick's stint in net marked the last time he played and won a Cup—21 years after his first championship as a star forward with the Montreal Wanderers in 1907.

7.11 **B. Bruce MacGregor**

Brad Park and Brian Propp are the first NHLers who come to mind when tallying up the most frustrated NHLers without a Cup. Park's Hall of Fame career included numerous All-Star appearances and 161 postseason matches, but no silver chalice. Propp, at 160, managed one less playoff game than Park, but he has more goals (64) than any other postseason performer without a Cup. Although Dale Hunter has more to complain about than anyone, with 186 fruitless playoff games, he is a less likely choice considering he had one chance in a final—with Washington in 1998—during his lengthy 19-year career. The surprise is the Cup-less Bruce MacGregor, way back of the pack with 107 playoff contests but a league-high 30 appearances in the finals. MacGregor's string of frustration began with his first career goal, a playoff game-winner that tied Detroit and Chicago 2–2 in the 1961 finals. The Blackhawks won the next two matches and the Cup, ushering in the MacGregor curse on playoff-bound teams. Each of his five finals series ended in failure, but earned MacGregor this dubious distinction after 24 final games with Detroit and six with New York. Propp is second with 29 and Norm Ullman has 28.

7.12   **A. In the 1964 playoffs**

They're a sensitive and superstitious bunch those Boston fans, but there may be something to their "Canadiens Hex," a bit of postseason hocus-pocus concocted by the hockey gods to curse any club that beats Montreal in the early rounds. After seeing his beloved Bruins lose for the fourth time in five years after eliminating the Canadiens, tortured fan Dave Bontempo discovered statistical evidence that he believed was more than coincidental. On 19 consecutive occasions, winners over Montreal were later defeated in the playoffs. "Do teams suffer a letdown after defeating the Canadiens in a playoff series?" Bontempo asked in a Montreal *Gazette* story. "Or is defeating the Canadiens like winning the Stanley Cup in a figurative sense?" Good questions, considering the last Cup-winner to knock out Montreal before the finals was the Toronto Maple Leafs in 1964. The Lightning only broke the hex with their Cup victory in 2004.

7.13 B. The Calgary Flames

Born out of the improbable season that led to Calgary's stunning run at the Stanley Cup finals in 2004, the hard hat honours the Flames' hardest-working player each game— awarded by the players themselves to one of their peers. The tradition took off among Flames fans as Calgary moved deeper into the playoffs that year. The hard hat is one of several franchise traditions among hockey fans, including the throwing of octopi in Detroit, the waving of white towels in Vancouver and the now-banned practice of tossing plastic rats in Florida.

7.14 C. Seven shutouts

The New Jersey Devils earned each of their three Stanley Cups with a winning combination of timely offense, killer defense and the stellar netminding of Martin Brodeur. During the 2003 playoff run, the hockey wasn't particularly entertaining or compelling as the Devils' "D" choked the life out of its opponents with traps, dump-ins and dump-outs. But it won the day as Brodeur netted an unheard of seven shutouts in a 16-victory march to the Cup. Despite Brodeur's magnificent play, however, the Conn Smythe Trophy was awarded to playoff MVP and final series loser Jean-Sebastien Giguere, who himself recorded five shutouts with Anaheim. Brodeur had shutouts in each series: two against Boston, one versus Tampa Bay and Ottawa and three to blank the Ducks in the final round.

7.15 D. Brad Richards of the Tampa Bay Lightning (in 2004)

The pride of Murray Harbour, Prince Edward Island, Brad Richards earned his Conn Smythe Trophy in 2004 with an MVP-worthy performance, scoring a postseason-leading

26 points, including 12 goals and a record-setting seven game-winners. Richards's uncanny talent for scoring the goals that matter most began in Game 3 of the first round against the New York Islanders. He then scored the deciding goals in Games 3 and 4 of the second-round sweep of Montreal and Games 1 and 5 against Philadelphia in the Tampa Bay's first Conference finals. In the Cup's final series, he tied Joe Sakic's record of six game-winners in the Lightning's 4–1 win in Game 2 and netted his record seventh in Game 4, when Tampa Bay evened the series at two in its 1–0 win against Calgary. Richards also led all players in the playoffs in average ice time per game, with 23:28.

7.16   A. The Edmonton Oilers

For most teams, the Stanley Cup finals are the height of their success, not a stepping stone to greater glory the following spring. History has not been kind to finalists, who most often find themselves further away from a championship come the next playoff year. Chicago is still waiting for a return to the big dance since the 1992 finals, as is Los Angeles (1993), Vancouver (1994), Florida (1996), Washington (1998), Buffalo (1999) and Anaheim (2003). As of 2005, the last team to break the bridesmaid curse is the Cup-winning Edmonton Oilers, who in 1984 avenged four straight losses to the New York Islanders in the 1983 Cup finals.

7.17   D. He asked Gretzky himself for it

It was a gutsy move by anyone's standards, never mind that the request for Gretzky's silver Easton hockey stick came from an opponent who only moments earlier had snatched victory at the 1993 Stanley Cup finals. And, the appeal was from that same man who outed Marty McSorley in Game 2 for using an illegal stick, a penalty that turned the series in Montreal's favour. But Jacques Demers, who had known Gretzky since their WHA days, asked anyway. Montreal was jubilantly celebrating its 24th Stanley Cup and the two men were shaking hands in the customary lineup after the game, and the Great One graciously obliged. It turned out to be Gretzky's last stick from a Stanley Cup game.

7.18   A. Only one goal

Much like baseball's Pete Rose, Wayne Gretzky kept close tabs on his personal statistics and the scoring records he was in range of breaking. But before he retired at the end of the 1998–99 season, Gretzky made sure he set another prestigious, though unpublicized, milestone. By notching goal number 1,072 on March 29, 1999, against the New York Islanders, the Great One surpassed Gordie Howe's mark for most goals as a professional, including playoff games. It was Gretzky's last goal as a professional and it left him one up on Mr. Hockey, who racked up 869 NHL goals and another 202 in the WHA. Gretzky amassed 1,016 NHL goals plus an additional 56 during his lone season in the WHA.

Solutions to Games

Game 1: The Third Jersey

1. E. NYR; The *Statue of Liberty*'s head
2. F. Calgary; Horse head snorting fire
3. K. Columbus; A star, wrapped in the Ohio State flag
4. J. Ottawa; A Roman's head, looking out
5. I. Edmonton; Drop of oil in a gear-like design
6. H. Los Angeles; Coat of arms
7. G. Montreal; Replica of a 1945 jersey
8. B. Nashville; Sabre-tooth tiger protruding out of a triangle
9. A. Boston; Brown bear
10. D. Dallas; Bull's head with a star constellation
11. C. Toronto; Replica of a 1938 jersey

Game 2: Lockout Lingo

PART 1

1. Flyers goalie Robert Esche, a vocal opponent to the salary cap, later apologized for calling Gary Bettman a "madman"
2. TV host Jay Leno
3. Wayne Gretzky, on his and Mario Lemieux's attempt to help negotiations between players and management
4. Ottawa enforcer Rob Ray, on why he would be happy to be a replacement player, one of the first to make such a damning comment in October 2004
5. Former NHL great Marcel Dionne
6. Mike Lupica, the *New York Daily News*, on the poor-performing, high-salaried Ranger players
7. L.A. Kings forward Sean Avery, on the way negotiations were conducted and the results

PART 2

1. Bob Goodenow
2. Jim Armstrong, the *Denver Post*
3. All-time minor-league goal leader Kevin Kerr, on playing as a replacement player if he were asked
4. Flyers GM Bobby Clarke, on NHLPA president Bob Goodenow

5. Greg Cote, the *Miami Herald*
6. New Jersey's general manager Lou Lamoriello, using the death of Pope John Paul II as an analogy
7. Gary Bettman, making it clear replacement players would not be used

Game 3: The Triggermen

PART 1

1. C. Ilya Kovalchuk; 341 shots in 2003–04
2. B. Darryl Sittler; 311 shots in 1977–78
3. A. Ray Bourque; 340 shots in 1983–84
4. G. Brett Hull; 408 shots in 1991–92
5. E. Pavel Bure; 384 shots in 2000–01
6. D. Paul Kariya; 429 shots in 1998–99
7. F. Bobby Orr; 384 shots in 1974–75

PART 2

1. E. Phil Esposito; 550 shots in 1970–71
2. F. Bill Guerin; 355 shots in 2001–02
3. C. Brendan Shanahan; 397 shots in 1993–94
4. A. Marcel Dionne; 348 shots in 1979–80
5. G. Jaromir Jagr; 403 shots in 1995–96
6. D. Bobby Hull; 364 shots in 1967–68
7. B. Wayne Gretzky; 369 shots in 1981–82

Game 4: The Best Rookie Class Ever?

1. Alexander Ovechkin set an NHL rookie record with 425 shots on goal, topping Teemu Selanne's mark of 387 in 1992–93.
2. Josh Harding is the first goalie to play his first NHL game and record his first win in a shootout. It happened in Minnesota's 5–4 win against the St. Louis Blues on April 4, 2006.
3. Sidney Crosby became the youngest player in NHL history to score 90 points on April 7, 2006, when he notched four points against the Florida Panthers. He was 18 years and 243 days old, 100 days younger than Dale Hawerchuk, who hit 90 points at the age of 18 years, 343 days, during his remarkable rookie year, 1982–83. Then, on April 17, Crosby set up three goals in a 6–1 win against the Islanders to reach his 100th point. He was three months younger than Hawerchuk. Only Wayne Gretzky was this good so young; and Gretzky was in the WHA.

4. Dion Phaneuf is only the third rookie defenseman to reach the 20-goal plateau in one season. He did it on April 13, 2006, versus the Colorado Avalanche.

5. Alexander Ovechkin is the second rookie in NHL history to record 50 goals and 100 points in one season. In 2005–06, he amassed 52 goals and 54 assists for 106 points, compared to Teemu Selanne's 76–56–132 in his first season, 1992–93.

6. Henrik Lundqvist set the New York Rangers record for most wins by a rookie goalie on March 29, 2006, when he made 18 saves in a 5–1 win over the New York Islanders. It was his 30th win, the most by a Ranger goalie since Mike Richter in 1996–97.

7. Alexander Ovechkin is the first rookie to lead an NHL regular season in shots on goal, with 425 in 2005–06.

8. Marek Svatos tied the NHL rookie record with nine game-winning goals in one season, set by Steve Larmer in 1982–83. His nine game-winners for Colorado led the entire NHL at the time of his season-ending shoulder injury March 4 in Dallas. At that point, only Alexander Ovechkin had more than Svatos's 32 goals and only Ovechkin and Sidney Crosby had more points among first-year players.

9. Sidney Crosby is second in most points by a rookie who entered the league in the same year he was drafted, behind only Dale Hawerchuk's 103 points in 1981–82. Crosby netted 102 points in 2005–06.

10. Jussi Jokinen led all players with 10 shootout goals in 13 attempts during 2005–06, the first shootout year in the NHL.

11. Kari Lehtonen of the Atlanta Thrashers had the best save-percentage in shootouts, stopping 17 of 20 shots for .850.

12. Alexander Ovechkin is only the fourth rookie in NHL history to reach the 50-goal mark in one season, after Teemu Selanne, Mike Bossy and Joe Nieuwendyk.

13. Ottawa's Ray Emery posted a 12–2–2 record in March 2006, tying Bernie Parent's mark of 12 wins in a calendar month, March 1974.

14. As 100-point earners, Alexander Ovechkin (106) and Sidney Crosby (102) produced two NHL firsts. It was the first time that two rookies scored 100 points and that two rookies finished top 10 in scoring.

15. Henrik Lundqvist (30), Ryan Miller (30), Antero Niittymaki (23). Ray Emery (23) and Kari Lehtonen (20) equalled the league record set in 1981–82 for most rookie netminders posting 20 or more victories.

Game 5: NHL Olympians

1. J. Nik Antropov, Toronto; Team Kazakhstan
2. K. Tomas Vokoun, Nashville; Team Czech Republic
3. F. Todd Bertuzzi, Vancouver; Team Canada
4. C. Olaf Kolzig, Washington; Team Germany
5. A. Olli Jokinen, Florida; Team Finland
6. G. Zdeno Chara, Ottawa; Team Slovakia
7. H. Karlis Strastins, Colorado; Team Latvia
8. B. Pavel Datysyuk, Detroit; Team Russia
9. E. Fredrik Modin, Tampa Bay; Team Sweden
10. I. Mark Streit, Montreal; Team Switzerland
11. D. Chris Drury, Buffalo; Team USA

Game 6: Chris Who?

PART 1

1. C. Chris Dingman; Tampa Bay Lightning, 2004
2. E. Jiri Fischer; Detroit Red Wings, 2002
3. F. Kevin Haller; Montreal Canadiens, 1993
4. D. Hector Marini; New York Islanders, 1982
5. B. Troy Loney; Pittsburgh Penguins, 1992
6. A. Craig Muni; Edmonton Oilers, 1988

PART 2

1. D. Colin Patterson; Calgary Flames, 1989
2. B. Ace Bailey: Boston Bruins, 1972
3. E. Dave Reid; Dallas Stars, 1999
4. F. Jay Pandolfo; New Jersey Devils, 2003
5. A. Dan Hinote; Colorado Avalanche, 2001
6. C. Brian Noonan; New York Rangers, 1994

Acknowledgements

Thanks to the following publishers and organizations for the use of quoted and statistical material:

- The *Hockey News,* various excerpts. Reprinted with the permission of the *Hockey News,* a division of GTC Transcontinental Publishing, Inc.

- *The Official NHL Guide and Record Book.* Published by Total Sports Canada.

- *Total Hockey,* second edition; *Total Stanley Cup* (1998, 2000); and *Total NHL* (2003) by Dan Diamond and Associates Inc. Published by Total Sports. 1998, 2000.

- The Associated Press; the *Dallas Morning News; Esquire* magazine; the *Globe and Mail;* ITAR-Tass news agency; *Jacques Demers: Toutes en Lettres;* the *Los Angeles Daily News;* the *Montreal Gazette;* NBC *News;* the *National Post;* the Newark *Star-Ledger;* the *Ottawa Citizen; Sports Illustrated; USA Today,* and numerous other books and publications that both guided and corroborated our research.

Care has been taken to trace ownership of copyright material contained in this book. The publishers welcome any information that will enable them to rectify any reference or credit in subsequent editions.

The author gratefully acknowledges all the help throughout the years from Jason Kay and everyone at the *Hockey News;* Gary Meagher and Benny Ercolani of the NHL; Phil Prichard and Craig Campbell at the Hockey Hall of Fame; the staff at the McLellan-Redpath Library at

McGill University; Rob Sanders and Susan Rana at Greystone Books; designer Lisa Hemingway; the many hockey writers, broadcast-journalists, media and Internet organizations who have made the game better through their own work; statistical resources such as the Elias Sports Bureau, NHL.com, hockeydb.com, CBC.com, eurosport.com, HHF.com and shrpsports.com; and inputter Bev Jang and editor Anne Rose for their dedication, expertise and creativity. Finally, special thanks to Kerry Banks for all of his contributions along the way.